Deep Learning

AI Foundations

Deep Learning

AI Foundations

Sergio Ramirez Gallardo

Index

1. Introduction to Deep Learning   11

   1.1. Definition and Relevance in Modern AI   11

   1.2. Comparison with Classical Machine Learning Techniques 12

2. Origins of Neural Networks   15

   2.1. History of AI and Deep Learning   15

   2.2. Evolution of Neural Networks   16

   2.3. Importance of Research and Development   17

   2.4. Conclusions   17

3. Fundamental Principles   19

   3.1. Biological and Theoretical Inspiration   19

   3.2. Basic Structure of an Artificial Neuron   20

   3.3. Conclusions   21

4. Introduction to TensorFlow   23

   4.1. What is TensorFlow?   23

   4.2. Installation and Setup   24

4.3. Getting Started with TensorFlow   25

4.4. Building a Basic Model   27

4.5. Conclusions   30

5. Introduction to PyTorch   31

5.1. What is PyTorch?   31

5.2. Installation and Setup   32

5.3. Getting Started with PyTorch   33

5.4. Building a Basic Model   35

5.5. Predictions   39

5.6. Conclusions   39

6. The Perceptron   41

6.1. Concept and Functioning   41

6.2. Limitations of the Simple Perceptron   44

6.3. Conclusions   45

7. Multilayer Neural Networks   47

7.1. Architecture and Functionality   47

7.2. Functioning of a Multilayer Neural Network   48

7.3. Example Implementation of a Multilayer Neural Network   50

7.4. Conclusions   52

8. Activation Functions   53

8.1. What is an Activation Function?   53

8.2. Main Activation Functions   54

8.3. Choosing the Activation Function   57

8.4. Example Implementation of Activation Functions   58

8.5. Conclusions   59

9. Data Normalization   61

9.1. Importance of Normalization   61

9.2. Normalization Techniques   62

9.3. Considerations When Normalizing   65

9.4. Conclusion   65

10. Backpropagation Algorithm   67

10.1. What is the Backpropagation Algorithm?   67

10.2. Backpropagation Process   68

10.3. Backpropagation Implementation Example in Python   70

10.4. Importance of the Backpropagation Algorithm   72

10.5. Conclusions   73

11. Gradient Descent Methods   75

11.1. What is Gradient Descent?   75

11.2. Types of Gradient Descent   76

11.3. Learning Rate   78

11.4. Variants of Gradient Descent   79

11.5. Implementation Example in Python   80

11.6. Conclusions   81

12. Introduction to Convolutional Neural Networks   83

12.1. What are Convolutional Neural Networks?   83

12.2. Structure of a Convolutional Network   84

12.3. Training Process of a Convolutional Network   86

12.4. Example Implementation of a CNN in Python   87

12.5. Applications of Convolutional Neural Networks   89

12.6. Final Considerations   89

13. Convolution Operations   91

13.1. What is Convolution?   91

13.2. Convolution Process   92

13.3. Stride and Padding   93

13.4. Example of Convolution in Python 93

13.5. Differences Between Convolution and Correlation 95

13.6. Applications of Convolution 96

13.7. Conclusions 96

14. Fundamentals of Recurrent Networks 97

14.1. What are Recurrent Neural Networks? 97

14.2. Architecture of an RNN 98

14.3. Calculating the Hidden State 99

14.4. Common Problems in RNNs 99

14.5. Applications of RNNs 100

14.6. Long Short-Term Memory (LSTM) 101

14.7. Gated Recurrent Unit (GRU) 102

14.8. Example of RNN Implementation in Python 102

14.9. Conclusions 105

15. Long Short-Term Memory (LSTM) 107

15.1. LSTM Architecture 107

15.2. Advantages of LSTMs 110

15.3. Applications of LSTMs 110

15.4. LSTM Implementation Example in Python 111

15.5. Conclusions 114

16. Transformer Architecture 115

16.1. What is a Transformer? 115

16.2. Fundamentals of the Transformer Architecture 116

16.3. Attention Mechanism 117

16.4. Positional Encoding 119

16.5. Applications of Transformers 119

16.6. Example Implementation of a Transformer in Python 120

16.7. Conclusions 123

17. Generative Models 125

17.1. What are Generative Models? 125

17.2. Generative Adversarial Networks (GANs) 126

17.3. Applications of GANs 128

17.4. Example of Implementing a GAN in Python 130

18. Optimization Techniques 135

18.1. Basic Concepts of Optimization 135

18.2. Gradient and Gradient Descent 136

18.3. Advanced Optimization Algorithms 139

18.4. Learning Strategies 141

18.5. Implementing an Optimization Algorithm in Python 142

18.6. Conclusions 143

19. Regularization 145

19.1. What is Overfitting? 145

19.2. Regularization Techniques 146

19.3. Implementing Regularization in Python 148

19.4. Conclusions 151

20. Natural Language Processing I 153

20.1. Introduction to Natural Language Processing 153

20.2. Text Representation for Neural Networks 154

20.3. Basic Models for NLP 156

20.4. Problems and Limitations of RNNs 158

20.5. Conclusions 158

21. Natural Language Processing II 159

21.1. Transformers and Their Impact on NLP 159

21.2. Modern Language Models 160

21.3. Advanced Techniques in NLP 162

21.4. Practical Applications in NLP   163

21.5. Implementing Modern Models in Python   164

21.6. Conclusions   165

22. Computer Vision I   167

22.1. Introduction to Computer Vision   167

22.2. Image Representation in Neural Networks   169

22.3. Convolutional Neural Networks (CNNs)   170

22.4. Example Implementation of a CNN in Python   172

22.5. Conclusions   174

23. Computer Vision II   175

23.1. Improving Performance with Transfer Learning and Fine-Tuning   175

23.2. Advanced Models: ResNet and DenseNet   177

23.3. Object Detection   180

23.4. Implementation of YOLO in Python   181

23.5. Conclusions   183

24. Ethical Considerations   185

24.1. Social and Economic Impacts   185

24.2. Biases in Machine Learning Models   186

24.3. The Need for Responsible AI   188

24.4. Conclusions   189

25. Technical Challenges and the Future of Deep Learning   191

25.1. Current Limitations of the Technology   191

25.2. Future Trends in Deep Learning   193

25.3. The Role of Ethics in the Future of Deep Learning   195

25.4. Conclusions   195

Introduction to Deep Learning

Deep Learning is one of the most important and revolutionary branches of modern artificial intelligence (AI). This technique has enabled significant advances in various areas such as computer vision, machine translation, and natural language processing, among others. In this chapter, we will explore the definition and relevance of deep learning, as well as how it compares with other classical machine learning techniques.

Definition and Relevance in Modern AI

Deep learning is a subfield of machine learning that uses artificial neural networks to model and solve complex problems. These neural networks are composed of multiple layers of nodes (neurons) that transform data as it progresses through the network. Each layer learns to extract features from the data, and at each level of abstraction, the representations become more complex and useful.

Unlike more traditional machine learning techniques, which require manual feature engineering, deep learning allows models to automatically discover these features from raw data. This is particularly useful in tasks where data is hard to structure, such as images or text.

The relevance of deep learning can be observed in several recent accomplishments. For instance, convolutional neural networks (CNNs) have surpassed human performance in image recognition tasks, while language models based on the Transformer architecture have dramatically improved the capabilities of machine translation and text generation.

Comparison with Classical Machine Learning Techniques

To understand how deep learning distinguishes itself from classical machine learning techniques, it is useful to compare their approaches:

- **Feature Engineering vs. Feature Learning**: In classical techniques, such as decision trees or SVM (Support Vector Machine), the data engineer must identify and extract relevant features from the data before training a model. This process can be tedious and subjective. In contrast, deep learning automates this task by allowing the model to learn directly from large amounts of data without human intervention in feature extraction.

- **Model Depth**: Classical models are often limited to a few levels of processing. For instance, a decision tree can only make decisions based on a set of features at one time. On the other hand, deep neural networks can have hundreds of layers, enabling them to create hierarchical representations and capture complex patterns in data.

- **Data Requirements**: Classical learning techniques generally require less data to train efficiently, while deep learning significantly benefits from large volumes of data. This is because a deep model has a greater number of parameters that need to be learned, which necessitates more information to avoid issues like overfitting.

- **Generalization Capability**: Often, deep learning models tend to generalize better on very complex tasks. However, they are more susceptible to needing fine-tuning of hyperparameters and regularization techniques to deliver optimal performance.

In summary, deep learning provides a powerful and scalable way to address complex problems, especially in contexts where data is rich and diverse. As we will see in subsequent chapters, this methodology has set new standards in how we approach and solve problems in the field of artificial intelligence.

In the following sections, we will begin to delve into the origins and foundations of neural networks, to better understand how this fascinating field evolves and why it is an essential pillar in modern artificial intelligence.

Origins of Neural Networks

The history of neural networks is a fascinating journey through decades of scientific and technological advancements. From their early conceptions in the 1940s to the impressive current applications in artificial intelligence, this chapter will explore the evolution of neural networks and their crucial role in the development of deep learning.

History of AI and Deep Learning

Artificial intelligence as a field of study began in the 1950s when visionary researchers started to formulate theories on how machines could imitate human behavior. One of the early milestones was the creation of the "Turing machine" by Alan Turing, which established the theoretical foundations for modern computing and the ability of machines to solve problems.

In the 1940s, Warren McCulloch and Walter Pitts presented a model of an artificial neuron in their 1943 paper, proposing a system that could transmit signals similarly to how the human brain functions. This model was based on the idea that neurons in the brain respond to stimuli and can activate other neurons, forming complex networks.

However, it was in 1958 when Frank Rosenblatt introduced the perceptron, a simple neural network model that could learn to classify patterns from examples. Although the perceptron was a significant advancement, it had limitations: it could only solve linearly separable problems. This led to a phase of stagnation in neural network research in the following decades, known as the "AI winter."

Evolution of Neural Networks

Starting in the 1980s, a renaissance of neural networks began when scientists like Geoffrey Hinton and Yann LeCun developed more advanced learning algorithms. In 1986, Hinton, alongside David Parker, presented the backpropagation algorithm, which enabled the effective training of multilayer neural networks. This method addressed the limitation of the simple perceptron by allowing weight adjustments in more complex networks, opening the door to a new world of possibilities for machine learning.

In the 1990s, interest in neural networks again waned due to the popularity of simpler and more efficient algorithms, such as decision trees and support vector machines. However, by the mid-2000s, the availability of large volumes of data, alongside advances in computational power (especially GPUs), revitalized the field of neural networks. Researchers began experimenting with deeper and more sophisticated architectures.

The term "deep learning" started to gain popularity in 2006 when Geoffrey Hinton published a key paper on the use of hidden layers in neural networks. With the resurgence of interest, more complex architectures were developed, such as convolutional networks (CNNs) for computer vision and recurrent networks (RNNs) for sequence processing.

Importance of Research and Development

The evolution of neural networks would not have been possible without contributions from numerous disciplines, such as neuroscience, statistics, and information theory. Understanding the human brain has provided valuable insights into how to design more efficient neural networks. For example, studying how neurons communicate and how synaptic connections are organized has influenced how neural networks are structured and trained.

A notable milestone in the history of neural networks occurred with the significant advancement in image classification in 2012, when Alex Krizhevsky, Ilya Sutskever, and Geoffrey Hinton won the ImageNet competition with their network called AlexNet. This model employed deep learning techniques that dazzled the community, achieving a 15% improvement over the second place. This triumph catapulted deep learning into the spotlight, and since then, substantial investments have been made in research and development in this field.

Conclusions

The history of neural networks is a testament to human ingenuity and perseverance in the pursuit of understanding and replicating intelligence processes. From the simplest models to the sophisticated architectures that drive the current revolution in artificial intelligence, the path has been filled with challenges and valuable discoveries.

As we progress through this book, we will explore the fundamental principles and techniques that build upon this rich history, starting with the understanding of the perceptron and multilayer neural networks in the next chapter. These concepts will serve as the cornerstone for unraveling the secrets behind modern deep learning and its impact on the present and future of artificial intelligence.

Fundamental Principles

Deep learning is based on a series of fundamental principles inspired by how the human brain functions. Throughout this chapter, we will explore the biological inspiration behind neural networks, the basic structure of an artificial neuron, and how these elements contribute to the effective functioning of deep learning models.

Biological and Theoretical Inspiration

Neural networks are inspired by the human brain, which is composed of trillions of interconnected neurons. Each neuron receives signals from other neurons, processes these signals, and then transmits an impulse through its connection to other neurons. This system of interconnections allows the brain to perform complex tasks such as perception, reasoning, and learning.

In an artificial neural network, the nodes (or neurons) are points in a network that perform simple mathematical functions. Although these artificial neurons do not precisely replicate the complexity of the human brain, they are capable of learning patterns and relationships in data through weighted connections. The weights, which represent the strength of the connection between neurons, are adjusted during the training process, allowing the network to learn from examples.

Basic Structure of an Artificial Neuron

An artificial neuron has a fairly simple structure, but it is fundamental to the functioning of neural networks. Let's look at its components:

1. **Inputs**: Neurons receive a series of inputs. These can be raw data, such as pixel values in an image or features extracted in a machine learning context.

2. **Weights**: Each input is multiplied by a weight, which determines the importance of that input in the neuron's activation process. This step can be mathematically represented as:

$$z = \sum_{i=1}^{n} w_i \cdot x_i$$

where z is the weighted sum of the inputs, w_i are the weights, and x_i are the inputs.

3. **Activation Function**: After calculating the weighted sum (often referred to as "z"), the neuron applies an activation function to this result. The activation function decides whether the neuron "fires" or not, transforming the weighted sum into a non-linear output. There are various activation functions, including the sigmoid function, ReLU (Rectified Linear Unit), and tanh (hyperbolic tangent).

4. **Output**: Finally, the neuron generates an output that can be used as input for neurons in the next layer of the network or as part of the model's final prediction.

With multiple layers of these neurons connected to each other, neural networks can learn complex and hierarchical representations of the data.

Example Implementation of an Artificial Neuron

Below is a small example in Python that demonstrates how to create a basic neuron with its inputs, weights, and an activation function.

```python
1   import numpy as np
2
3   # Definition of the activation function (ReLU)
4   def relu(x):
5       return max(0, x)
6
7   # Input data (example)
8   inputs = np.array([0.5, 0.3, 0.2])   # Input values
9   weights = np.array([0.4, 0.6, 0.1])   # Associated weights
10
11  # Calculation of the weighted sum
12  z = np.dot(weights, inputs)   # Dot product
13
14  # Application of the activation function
15  output = relu(z)
16
17  print(f"Weighted sum: {z}")
18  print(f"Neuron output: {output}")
```

In this example, we define a ReLU activation function, create a set of inputs and weights, calculate the weighted sum, and finally apply the activation function to obtain the neuron's output.

Conclusions

The fundamentally biological principles of neural networks, although simplified, allow us to model complex problems through a combination of interconnected neurons that learn patterns from data. Artificial neurons, with their basic structures and activation processes, are the cornerstone upon which advanced deep learning models are built.

In the next chapter, we will explore the perceptron, a basic neural network model that lays the foundation for understanding how multilayer neural networks operate and how we can overcome their initial limitations. This journey will allow us to delve deeper into the world of deep learning and its applications in artificial intelligence.

Introduction to TensorFlow

TensorFlow is one of the most popular and powerful libraries for the development and implementation of machine learning and deep learning models. Developed by Google, TensorFlow provides a flexible and scalable infrastructure to build and train neural networks, along with tools for performing inference and optimizing model performance. In this chapter, we will explore TensorFlow from the basic concepts, installation, and configuration to building a basic model so that readers can begin experimenting with this powerful tool.

What is TensorFlow?

TensorFlow is an open-source library created to facilitate the creation of neural networks and deep learning algorithms. The term "TensorFlow" comes from its capabilities to handle tensors, which are multidimensional data structures. At its core, TensorFlow eases the flow of data through computational graphs, where each node in the graph represents a mathematical operation and the edges represent the tensors that flow between them.

TensorFlow is widely used in areas such as computer vision, natural language processing, speech recognition, and many other artificial intelligence-related applications. Its flexibility and scalability make it suitable for both research and production.

Installation and Setup

Prerequisites

Before starting to work with TensorFlow, it is essential to have Python installed on your system. TensorFlow is compatible with Python 3.7 or higher. It is also recommended to have `pip` installed, which is the package management system for Python.

Installing TensorFlow

The easiest way to install TensorFlow is through `pip`. You can install the latest stable version of TensorFlow with the following command:

```
1  pip install tensorflow
```

If you want to take advantage of GPU processing capabilities, you can install the GPU-optimized version of TensorFlow. Make sure your system has the appropriate GPU drivers and CUDA installed. The installation can be done with:

```
1  pip install tensorflow-gpu
```

Verifying the Installation

After installation, it is important to verify that TensorFlow has been installed correctly. You can do this by opening a Python interpreter and importing the library:

```
1  import tensorflow as tf
2  print(tf.__version__)
```

If you see the version of TensorFlow without errors, congratulations! TensorFlow is installed and ready to use.

Getting Started with TensorFlow

Once TensorFlow is installed, it's time to take our first steps. We will start with creating and manipulating tensors, which are fundamental elements in TensorFlow.

Creating Tensors

Tensors in TensorFlow are similar to NumPy arrays but can be used in computational graphs. Here's a basic way to create tensors:

```
1  import tensorflow as tf
2
3  # Create a constant tensor
4  tensor_c = tf.constant([[1, 2], [3, 4]])
5
6  # Create a random tensor
7  tensor_random = tf.random.uniform(shape=(2, 3), minval=0,
```

```
    maxval=10)
 8
 9  # Create a tensor from a list
10  tensor_from_list = tf.Variable([[1, 2, 3], [4, 5, 6]])
11
12  print(tensor_c)
13  print(tensor_random)
14  print(tensor_from_list)
```

Operations with Tensors

Basic operations on tensors are fundamental for data manipulation. TensorFlow allows operations such as addition, subtraction, multiplication, and transposition.

```
1  # Add tensors
2  tensor_sum = tf.add(tensor_c, tensor_from_list)
3
4  # Multiply tensors
5  tensor_product = tf.matmul(tensor_c, tf.transpose(
       tensor_from_list))
6
7  print(tensor_sum)
8  print(tensor_product)
```

Furthermore, TensorFlow allows more complex operations, such as reducing or creating masks. These operations are essential for manipulating data during model training.

Building a Basic Model

Next, we will build a simple neural network model using TensorFlow and Keras, a high-level API built on TensorFlow that simplifies the process of creating and training deep learning models.

Loading a Dataset

To illustrate the construction of a model, we will use the MNIST dataset, which contains images of handwritten digits. TensorFlow provides tools for loading common datasets.

```python
from tensorflow.keras.datasets import mnist

# Load data
(X_train, y_train), (X_test, y_test) = mnist.load_data()

# Normalize the data
X_train = X_train.astype('float32') / 255.0
X_test = X_test.astype('float32') / 255.0

# Reshape the data
X_train = X_train.reshape(-1, 28, 28, 1)
X_test = X_test.reshape(-1, 28, 28, 1)

# Check the dimensions of the dataset
print(X_train.shape, y_train.shape)
```

Creating the Model

Now that we have loaded and prepared the data, we can build a simple neural network model. We will start with an input layer, followed by hidden layers and an output layer that will use the softmax activation function.

```
1   from tensorflow.keras import layers, models
2
3   # Define the Sequential model
4   model = models.Sequential()
5
6   # Input layer
7   model.add(layers.Conv2D(32, (3, 3), activation='relu',
     input_shape=(28, 28, 1)))
8   model.add(layers.MaxPooling2D((2, 2)))
9
10  # Hidden layer
11  model.add(layers.Conv2D(64, (3, 3), activation='relu'))
12  model.add(layers.MaxPooling2D((2, 2)))
13
14  # Dense layer
15  model.add(layers.Flatten())
16  model.add(layers.Dense(64, activation='relu'))
17  model.add(layers.Dense(10, activation='softmax'))
    # Output layer
18
19  # Model summary
20  model.summary()
```

Compiling the Model

After defining the model architecture, it is essential to compile it. This involves specifying the loss function, the optimizer, and the metrics we want to monitor during training.

```
1   model.compile(optimizer='adam',
```

```
2                      loss='sparse_categorical_crossentropy',
3                      metrics=['accuracy'])
```

Training the Model

We train the model by feeding it our training data. We define how many epochs we want to train and the batch size.

```
1  model.fit(X_train, y_train, epochs=5, batch_size=32,
      validation_split=0.2)
```

Evaluating the Model

After training, we evaluate the model using the test set to see how it performs on unseen data.

```
1  test_loss, test_accuracy = model.evaluate(X_test, y_test)
2  print(f"Test accuracy: {test_accuracy:.4f}")
```

Predictions

Finally, we can use the trained model to make predictions on new images.

```
1  predictions = model.predict(X_test)
2  predicted_classes = tf.argmax(predictions, axis=1)
3
4  # Prediction for the first image in the test set
5  print(f"Prediction for the first image: {predicted_classes[0]
```

```
}")
```

Conclusions

TensorFlow is a powerful and versatile tool for developing machine learning and deep learning models. Throughout this chapter, we have covered everything from installation and setup to creating a simple model using the MNIST dataset. The capabilities of TensorFlow are vast and range from basic experiments to complex production deployments. As readers continue their journey into the world of deep learning, TensorFlow will become an invaluable resource in their repertoire, enabling the creation of sophisticated and effective models to address a variety of applications in artificial intelligence.

Introduction to PyTorch

PyTorch is one of the most popular libraries for developing deep learning models and has become a preferred tool in the artificial intelligence research and development community. It provides a flexible and dynamic platform that allows developers and data scientists to build, train, and deploy machine learning models efficiently. In this chapter, we will explore the fundamental concepts of PyTorch, its installation and setup, and take a first look at building basic models using this powerful library.

What is PyTorch?

PyTorch is an open-source library developed by Facebook that provides tools for machine learning and scientific computing. Its main appeal lies in its focus on dynamic computational graphs, which means it allows for the modification of the model structure on the fly, thus facilitating intuitive manipulation of models. This contrasts with other libraries, such as TensorFlow, which traditionally use a static graph approach.

One of the most notable features of PyTorch is its seamless integration with NumPy, making it easy and efficient to work with tensors and perform mathematical operations. The library is particularly effective for GPU computation, which greatly accelerates training deep learning models.

Installation and Setup

Prerequisites

Before you start using PyTorch, make sure you have Python installed, preferably version 3.6 or higher. It is also recommended to have `pip` or `conda`, which are package managers for installing Python libraries.

Installing PyTorch

The installation of PyTorch may vary depending on whether you want to use the CPU or GPU version. PyTorch provides a website where you can generate the installation command based on your operating system, Python version, and whether you want CUDA support (to use GPU).

To install PyTorch for CPU, you can use the following command:

```
pip install torch torchvision torchaudio
```

If you are using a GPU and want to take advantage of it, make sure you have CUDA installed, and use the appropriate command, which you can find on the official PyTorch site.

Verifying the Installation

Once you have installed PyTorch, it is crucial to verify that the installation was successful. Open a Python interpreter and try importing PyTorch:

```
1  import torch
2  print(torch.__version__)
```

If you don't encounter any errors and see the PyTorch version, you're ready to get started!

Getting Started with PyTorch

Now that you have PyTorch installed and running, we will begin exploring its basic usage, starting with the creation and manipulation of tensors.

Creating Tensors

Tensors are the basic data structure in PyTorch, similar to NumPy arrays but with the added capability of GPU computation. Below are some common examples of how to create tensors in PyTorch:

```
1  import torch
2
3  # Create a constant tensor
4  tensor_c = torch.tensor([[1, 2], [3, 4]])
5
6  # Create a random tensor
7  tensor_random = torch.rand((2, 3))
8
9  # Create a tensor of zeros
10 tensor_zeros = torch.zeros((3, 3))
11
12 # Create a tensor from a list
```

```
13  tensor_from_list = torch.tensor([[1, 2, 3], [4, 5, 6]])
14
15  print(tensor_c)
16  print(tensor_random)
17  print(tensor_zeros)
18  print(tensor_from_list)
```

Tensor Operations

Like in NumPy, PyTorch allows for basic mathematical operations on tensors such as addition, multiplication, and transposition. It also supports more advanced operations, and it is easy to perform operations on a tensor using the GPU.

Here are some examples of tensor operations:

```
1  # Tensor addition
2  tensor_sum = tensor_c + tensor_from_list
3
4  # Tensor multiplication
5  tensor_product = torch.matmul(tensor_c, tensor_from_list.T)
6
7  print(tensor_sum)
8  print(tensor_product)
```

Transferring Tensors between CPU and GPU

Once you have created your tensor, you can transfer it between the CPU and GPU in PyTorch. First, you need to check if a GPU is available.

34

```
1  # Check if there is a GPU in the system
2  device = torch.device("cuda" if torch.cuda.is_available()
   else "cpu")
3
4  # Create a tensor and move it to the GPU
5  tensor_gpu = tensor_c.to(device)
6  print(tensor_gpu)
```

Building a Basic Model

To illustrate the usage of PyTorch, we will construct a simple neural network model using the MNIST dataset, which contains images of handwritten digits. PyTorch allows for building models in a very intuitive way.

Loading the Dataset

PyTorch provides `torchvision`, a library that includes tools for loading popular datasets and performing transformations. Below, you will load the MNIST dataset.

```
1  from torchvision import datasets, transforms
2
3  # Transformations to normalize the data
4  transform = transforms.Compose([transforms.ToTensor(),
5                                   transforms.Normalize((0.5,)
   , (0.5,))])
6
7  # Load the MNIST dataset
8  train_dataset = datasets.MNIST(root='data', train=True,
   download=True, transform=transform)
9  test_dataset = datasets.MNIST(root='data', train=False,
```

```
                download=True, transform=transform)
10
11   # Create DataLoaders to handle the data during training
12   train_loader = torch.utils.data.DataLoader(dataset=
     train_dataset, batch_size=64, shuffle=True)
13   test_loader = torch.utils.data.DataLoader(dataset=
     test_dataset, batch_size=64, shuffle=False)
```

Defining the Model

We will use a simple feedforward neural network with two hidden layers. We will start by defining our model class.

```
1    import torch.nn as nn
2    import torch.nn.functional as F
3
4    class SimpleNN(nn.Module):
5        def __init__(self):
6            super(SimpleNN, self).__init__()
7            self.fc1 = nn.Linear(28 * 28, 128)  # Input layer
8            self.fc2 = nn.Linear(128, 64)         # Hidden layer
9            self.fc3 = nn.Linear(64, 10)          # Output layer
10
11       def forward(self, x):
12           x = x.view(-1, 28 * 28)  # Flatten input
13           x = F.relu(self.fc1(x))
     # Apply ReLU activation function
14           x = F.relu(self.fc2(x))  # Hidden layer
15           x = self.fc3(x)
     # Output layer without activation
16           return x
17
18   # Create an instance of the model
```

```
19  model = SimpleNN()
20  print(model)
```

Compiling the Model

In PyTorch, you do not need to compile the model in the same way you do in Keras. The training process is handled by defining the loss function and the optimizer, offering you more flexibility.

```
1  criterion = nn.CrossEntropyLoss()  # Loss function
2  optimizer = torch.optim.Adam(model.parameters(), lr=0.001)
       # Optimizer
```

Training the Model

In this section, we will train our model using the DataLoader we defined earlier. The training process includes forward propagation, loss calculation, and backpropagation.

```
1  # Training function
2  def train(model, train_loader, criterion, optimizer, epochs
   =5):
3      model.train()  # Set the model to training mode
4      for epoch in range(epochs):
5          for images, labels in train_loader:
6              optimizer.zero_grad()
           # Initialize gradients to zero
7              output = model(images)  # Forward propagation
8              loss = criterion(output, labels)
           # Calculate loss
```

```
9                     loss.backward()   # Backpropagation
10                    optimizer.step()  # Update parameters
11
12          print(f"Epoch {epoch + 1}, Loss: {loss.item():.4f}"
    )
13
14  # Run training
15  train(model, train_loader, criterion, optimizer)
```

Evaluating the Model

After training the model, it is important to evaluate it on the test set to measure its performance on unseen data.

```
1  def evaluate(model, test_loader):
2      model.eval()  # Set the model to evaluation mode
3      correct = 0
4      total = 0
5
6      with torch.no_grad():
    # Disable gradient calculation for efficiency
7          for images, labels in test_loader:
8              outputs = model(images)  # Predictions
9              _, predicted = torch.max(outputs.data, 1)
    # Class with highest probability
10             total += labels.size(0)  # Update total
11             correct += (predicted == labels).sum().item()
    # Count correct predictions
12
13      print(f'Model accuracy on the test set: {100 * correct
    / total:.2f}%')
14
15  # Evaluate the model
```

```
16  evaluate(model, test_loader)
```

Predictions

Finally, we can make predictions using the trained model. Here's how to predict the class of a specific image.

```python
1  # Make a prediction on the first image from the test set
2  image, label = test_dataset[0]
3  image = image.unsqueeze(0)  # Add a dimension for the batch
4  output = model(image)
5
6  # Print the predicted class
7  predicted_class = torch.argmax(output, dim=1)
8  print(f'Predicted class: {predicted_class.item()}
     , True class: {label}')
```

Conclusions

PyTorch is a powerful and flexible library that provides a wide range of tools for implementing machine learning and deep learning models. Throughout this chapter, we have covered everything from the installation and setup of PyTorch to the building, training, and evaluation of a basic model using the MNIST dataset. The simplicity and dynamics that PyTorch offers have made it a popular choice among researchers and developers in the field of artificial intelligence. As you continue to explore deep learning, PyTorch will become an invaluable resource for creating sophisticated and scalable models across a variety of applications.

The Perceptron

The perceptron is one of the simplest and most fundamental models in the history of machine learning and neural networks. Designed in the 1950s by Frank Rosenblatt, the perceptron has been a crucial starting point in the development of more advanced methods in artificial intelligence. In this chapter, we will explore the basic concept of the perceptron, how it works, the limitations it presents, and its historical contribution to the field.

Concept and Functioning

A perceptron is a type of neural network that consists of a single neuron. Its main function is to classify data into two distinct categories using a supervised learning process. The model takes several inputs, weights them, sums them, and then decides to which category that input belongs based on an activation function.

Let's take a detailed look at its components and the functioning process:

1. **Inputs**: The perceptron receives a vector of inputs, defined as

$x = [x_1, x_2, \ldots, x_n]$. These inputs can be features of the data that needs to be classified.

2. **Weights**: Each input has an associated weight, denoted as $w = [w_1, w_2, \ldots, w_n]$. The weights determine the importance of each input in the model's final prediction. A higher weight indicates that the corresponding input has more impact on the final decision.

3. **Weighted Sum**: The perceptron calculates a weighted sum of the inputs, mathematically expressed as:

$$z = \sum_{i=1}^{n} w_i \cdot x_i + b$$

where b is the bias, an additional term that allows the model to adjust the decision independently of the inputs.

4. **Activation Function**: The result of the weighted sum is passed through an activation function, which transforms z into a final output of 0 or 1, indicating to which class the input belongs. For a classic perceptron, the step activation function is used, defined as:

$$f(z) = \begin{cases} 1 & \text{if } z \geq 0 \\ 0 & \text{if } z < 0 \end{cases}$$

Example of Implementing a Perceptron

Below is a simple example of implementing a perceptron in Python. In this case, we will use a simple dataset to classify points in a two-dimensional space:

```
1   import numpy as np
2
3   class Perceptron:
4       def __init__(self, learning_rate=0.1, n_iterations=1000
```

```python
    ):
5           self.learning_rate = learning_rate
6           self.n_iterations = n_iterations
7           self.weights = None
8           self.bias = None
9
10      def fit(self, X, y):
11          n_samples, n_features = X.shape
12          # Initialize weights and bias
13          self.weights = np.zeros(n_features)
14          self.bias = 0
15
16          for _ in range(self.n_iterations):
17              for idx, x_i in enumerate(X):
18                  linear_output = np.dot(x_i, self.weights) +
    self.bias
19                  y_predicted = self.activation_function(
    linear_output)
20
21                  # Update weights and bias
22                  update = self.learning_rate * (y[idx] -
    y_predicted)
23                  self.weights += update * x_i
24                  self.bias += update
25
26      def activation_function(self, x):
27          return 1 if x >= 0 else 0
28
29      def predict(self, X):
30          linear_output = np.dot(X, self.weights) + self.bias
31          return np.array([self.activation_function(x) for x
    in linear_output])
32
33  # Example data
34  X = np.array([[0, 0], [0, 1], [1, 0], [1, 1]])  # Inputs
```

```
35  y = np.array([0, 0, 0, 1])  # Outputs - logical AND
36
37  # Creation and training of the model
38  model = Perceptron(learning_rate=0.1, n_iterations=10)
39  model.fit(X, y)
40
41  # Prediction
42  predictions = model.predict(X)
43  print(f'Predictions: {predictions}')
```

In this example, we created a `Perceptron` class that can be used to train a model using a dataset of four points representing the logical AND function. In the end, the model makes predictions based on the provided inputs.

Limitations of the Simple Perceptron

Despite being a fundamental model in artificial intelligence, the perceptron has several significant limitations:

1. **Non-Linearity**: The perceptron can only solve linearly separable problems. This means that it cannot adequately classify datasets that require a non-linear decision boundary. For example, it would be unable to solve problems like the XOR function, where the classes cannot be separated by a straight line in a two-dimensional space.

2. **Learning Capacity**: Being a model that only uses a single neuron, it lacks the capacity to learn more complex representations. This limits its application to problems requiring a higher level of abstraction.

3. **Convergence**: Although the perceptron converges to a solution for linearly separable data, it may not converge or take a long time if the data is very noisy or poorly distributed.

Conclusions

The perceptron is a key piece in the history of deep learning and has laid the groundwork for the development of multilayer neural networks and more complex models. Despite its limitations, its simplicity and effectiveness in certain types of problems make it relevant for understanding how neural networks function.

As we progress in this book, we will explore how multilayer neural networks overcome these limitations of the perceptron and how they can be trained to tackle more complex problems. The perceptron, though simple, is the first step on a journey toward more sophisticated and powerful architectures in the field of deep learning.

Multilayer Neural Networks

Multilayer neural networks (MLP) are a fundamental extension of the simple perceptron and represent one of the most important concepts in the field of deep learning. These complex structures allow models to learn highly sophisticated features of data through multiple levels of transformation. In this chapter, we will explore the architecture and functionality of multilayer neural networks, as well as how they can tackle problems that are beyond the capabilities of a single perceptron.

Architecture and Functionality

Structure of a Multilayer Neural Network

A multilayer neural network consists of a series of layers of neurons: the input layer, one or more hidden layers, and the output layer. Each of these layers contains several interconnected neurons. Let's break down each component:

1. **Input Layer**: This is the first layer of the network and is responsible for receiving input data. Each neuron in this layer corresponds to a feature of the dataset. For example, if our dataset consists of images, each neuron might represent the value of a pixel in the image.

2. **Hidden Layers**: These are the intermediate layers that process the information received from the input layer. Networks can have multiple hidden layers, and each layer learns to detect more complex patterns than the previous one. By using activation functions, each neuron in these layers applies nonlinear transformations to the signals it receives.

3. **Output Layer**: The last layer produces the final output of the network. In classification problems, this could be a probability vector indicating membership to each class; in regression problems, it would be a continuous value.

Connections and Weights

Neurons in different layers are interconnected, and each connection has an associated weight. These weights are what get adjusted during the training of the network. Information propagates from the input layer through the hidden layers to reach the output layer, and the weights determine the influence of each input on the final output.

When an input data point is presented to the network, each neuron in the input layer multiplies its input (the value of each feature) by the corresponding weight. This weighted sum is then passed to the next layer, where an activation function is applied.

Functioning of a Multilayer Neural Network

The functioning of a multilayer neural network can be divided into two phases: forward propagation and backward propagation. Let's explore each of these processes:

Forward Propagation

During the forward propagation phase, the information moves through the layers of the network. Each neuron calculates the weighted sum of its inputs and applies the activation function as follows:

1. **Calculating the weighted sum in a layer**:

$$z_j = \sum_i w_{ij} \cdot x_i + b_j$$

where z_j is the weighted sum for neuron j, w_{ij} is the weight of the connection between input i and neuron j, and b_j is the bias of the neuron.

2. **Applying the activation function**:

The output of the neuron is calculated using an activation function, which could be the sigmoid function, ReLU, tanh, among others.

$$a_j = f(z_j)$$

where a_j is the output of neuron j and f is the activation function.

This process is repeated across all layers until reaching the output layer, where the final predictions of the model are obtained.

Backward Propagation

Once forward propagation has been completed and an output has been obtained, it is compared with the expected output (true label or value) using a loss function. This measures how far the prediction is from the truth. The next step is to adjust the weights of the network to minimize this loss.

1. **Calculating the loss**:

    The loss function quantifies the discrepancy between the predictions of the network and the true values. For example, in the case of classification, cross-entropy can be used.

2. **Calculating gradients**:

    Using the backpropagation algorithm, the gradient of the loss function with respect to each weight in the network is calculated. This involves applying the chain rule, making use of the derivatives of the activation function and the loss function.

3. **Updating weights**:

    The weights are updated based on the calculated gradients. This is done using the gradient descent method:

    $$w_{ij} := w_{ij} - \eta \frac{\partial L}{\partial w_{ij}}$$

    where η is the learning rate and L is the loss function.

The backpropagation process is repeated over multiple iterations (epochs) to minimize the loss function.

Example Implementation of a Multilayer Neural Network

To illustrate how multilayer neural networks function, we will present a simple example using Python and the `Keras` library, which integrates with `TensorFlow`. This example will create a multilayer neural network to solve a classification problem using the iris dataset.

```
1   import numpy as np
```

```python
from tensorflow.keras.models import Sequential
from tensorflow.keras.layers import Dense
from sklearn.datasets import load_iris
from sklearn.model_selection import train_test_split
from sklearn.preprocessing import OneHotEncoder

# Load the iris dataset
iris = load_iris()
X = iris.data
y = iris.target.reshape(-1, 1)

# One-hot encoding for the labels
encoder = OneHotEncoder(sparse=False)
y_onehot = encoder.fit_transform(y)

# Split the dataset into training and testing sets
X_train, X_test, y_train, y_test = train_test_split(X,
 y_onehot, test_size=0.2, random_state=42)

# Create the multilayer neural network
model = Sequential()
model.add(Dense(10, input_dim=4, activation='relu'))
 # Hidden layer with 10 neurons
model.add(Dense(3, activation='softmax'))
 # Output layer with 3 neurons (one for each class)

# Compile the model
model.compile(loss='categorical_crossentropy', optimizer=
'adam', metrics=['accuracy'])

# Train the model
model.fit(X_train, y_train, epochs=100, batch_size=5,
 verbose=1)

# Evaluate the model on the testing set
```

```
32  loss, accuracy = model.evaluate(X_test, y_test)
33  print(f'Loss: {loss}, Accuracy: {accuracy}')
```

This code presents a simple multilayer neural network that learns to classify flower species from the iris dataset. It begins by loading the data, applying one-hot encoding to the labels, splitting into training and testing sets, and constructing the network using Keras. Finally, the model is trained and its accuracy is evaluated.

Conclusions

Multilayer neural networks have revolutionized the field of machine learning by allowing models to learn hierarchical representations of data. Their ability to handle complex patterns has enabled significant advancements in tasks that were previously difficult to tackle, such as computer vision and natural language processing.

As we continue to advance in this book, we will explore activation functions in detail along with other critical techniques that optimize the performance of multilayer neural networks. These tools are essential for understanding and improving deep learning models across various applications.

Activation Functions

Activation functions are fundamental components in the design of neural networks, as they determine how signals are transformed as they propagate through the layers of a network. Without activation functions, neural networks would behave similarly to a linear combination, eliminating their ability to learn complex patterns. In this chapter, we will explore what activation functions are, which ones are the most common, their characteristics, advantages and disadvantages, as well as considerations for choosing the appropriate function for a specific model.

What is an Activation Function?

An activation function is a mathematical function that decides whether a neuron should be activated or not, meaning whether it should transmit its information to the next layer of neurons. This function combines the weighted sum of the inputs and the bias of a neuron to produce a non-linear output. This non-linearity is crucial, as it allows the network to learn and model complicated relationships within the data.

Mathematically, if z is the weighted sum of a neuron's inputs, the output y is calculated as:

$$y = f(z)$$

where f is the activation function applied to z.

Main Activation Functions

Next, we will explore some of the most common activation functions and their applicability.

Sigmoid Function

The sigmoid function is one of the oldest activation functions. It is defined as:

$$f(z) = \frac{1}{1+e^{-z}}$$

Where e is the base of the natural logarithm. The sigmoid function produces an output between 0 and 1 and has an "S" shaped curve. It has the following characteristics:

- **Advantages**:

    - Its output is bounded, which can be useful for classification problems that require a result between 0 and 1.

    - It is differentiable, allowing for the use of gradient-based optimization methods.

- **Disadvantages**:

    - The "gradient vanishing" problem: as activations become

very high or very low, the derivative of the function approaches 0, which can hinder learning during training.

○ The output is not zero-centered, which can lead to issues in training.

Hyperbolic Tangent Function (tanh)

The hyperbolic tangent function is similar to the sigmoid function but produces values in the range of -1 to 1. It is defined as:

$$f(z) = \tanh(z) = \frac{e^z - e^{-z}}{e^z + e^{-z}}$$

- **Advantages**:

  ○ Being zero-centered, tanh can help balance activations during forward propagation, contributing to improved convergence.

  ○ The function is also differentiable and has better gradient propagation compared to the sigmoid function.

- **Disadvantages**:

  ○ Similar to the sigmoid function, the hyperbolic tangent also suffers from gradient vanishing for extreme values.

ReLU (Rectified Linear Unit)

The ReLU function is one of the most popular activation functions today due to its simplicity and efficiency. It is defined as:

$$f(z) = \max(0, z)$$

This means any negative value becomes 0, while positive values remain unchanged.

- **Advantages**:

    - The ReLU function does not activate neurons for negative values, making the network more efficient by reducing computations propagated forward.

    - It speeds up the training process as it avoids the gradient vanishing problem since its derivative is constant (1) for positive values.

- **Disadvantages**:

    - **Neuron death**: In some situations, neurons may completely stop learning if their outputs are always negative, meaning they "die" and never reactivate.

    - It can be sensitive to outliers, which may cause very large activations.

Variants of ReLU Functions

To mitigate some of the disadvantages of ReLU, variants have been developed, such as:

- **Leaky ReLU**:

$$f(z) = \begin{cases} z & \text{if } z > 0 \\ \alpha z & \text{if } z \leq 0 \end{cases}$$

where α is a small constant (for example, 0.01). This variant allows neurons to activate slightly even for negative inputs.

- **Parametric ReLU (PReLU)**: Similar to Leaky ReLU, but here α is a parameter that is trained during the learning process.

- **Exponential Linear Unit (ELU)**:

$$f(z) = \begin{cases} z & \text{if } z > 0 \\ \alpha(e^z - 1) & \text{if } z \leq 0 \end{cases}$$

The ELU has the advantage that its mean can approach zero, offering the possibility of enhanced convergence.

Softmax

The Softmax function is primarily used in the output layer of multi-class classification models. It converts logits (unnormalized output values) into probabilities that sum to 1. It is defined as:

$$f(z_i) = \frac{e^{z_i}}{\sum_j e^{z_j}}$$

Where z_i are the outputs from the previous layer. By using Softmax, the network can classify among several categories and obtain a result interpreted as probabilities.

Choosing the Activation Function

Choosing the appropriate activation function is crucial for the performance of a deep learning model. Some important points to consider include:

- **Nature of the Problem**: If it is a binary classification task, functions such as sigmoid or ReLU may be appropriate. For multi-class classification, Softmax should be used in the output layer.

- **Depth of the Network**: For deep networks, it is common to opt for functions like ReLU or its variants due to their better performance in practice.

- **Gradient Propagation**: It is important to consider how the choice of function will affect gradient propagation, especially in very deep networks.

Example Implementation of Activation Functions

Let's look at a brief example in Python that implements different activation functions. We will use `numpy` to handle the mathematical logic.

```python
1  import numpy as np
2  import matplotlib.pyplot as plt
3
4  # Definition of different activation functions
5  def sigmoid(z):
6      return 1 / (1 + np.exp(-z))
7
8  def tanh(z):
9      return np.tanh(z)
10
11 def relu(z):
12     return np.maximum(0, z)
13
14 def leaky_relu(z, alpha=0.01):
15     return np.where(z > 0, z, alpha * z)
16
17 # Range of values to plot
18 z = np.linspace(-10, 10, 100)
19
20 # Calculate outputs
21 sigmoid_output = sigmoid(z)
22 tanh_output = tanh(z)
23 relu_output = relu(z)
24 leaky_relu_output = leaky_relu(z)
25
```

```
26  # Plot
27  plt.figure(figsize=(12, 8))
28  plt.subplot(2, 2, 1)
29  plt.title("Sigmoid")
30  plt.plot(z, sigmoid_output, label='Sigmoid')
31  plt.grid()
32
33  plt.subplot(2, 2, 2)
34  plt.title("Tanh")
35  plt.plot(z, tanh_output, label='Tanh', color='orange')
36  plt.grid()
37
38  plt.subplot(2, 2, 3)
39  plt.title("ReLU")
40  plt.plot(z, relu_output, label='ReLU', color='green')
41  plt.grid()
42
43  plt.subplot(2, 2, 4)
44  plt.title("Leaky ReLU")
45  plt.plot(z, leaky_relu_output, label='Leaky ReLU', color=
    'purple')
46  plt.grid()
47
48  plt.tight_layout()
49  plt.show()
```

In this example, we define different activation functions and plot their outputs for a range of values from -10 to 10. This helps visualize how each function transforms the input z.

Conclusions

Activation functions play a crucial role in the effectiveness of neural networks, allowing models to learn complex patterns in the data. By selecting the right function, the performance and convergence of a network can be significantly improved. Throughout this chapter, we have learned about the main activation functions, their advantages and disadvantages, and how they influence the training of neural networks.

In the next chapter, we will analyze the importance of data normalization and how it lays the groundwork for the effective training of deep learning models.

Data Normalization

In the field of deep learning, properly handling data is crucial for the success of models. One of the most important steps in the data preparation process is normalization. This chapter will explore the importance of data normalization, the most common techniques used, and how this practice significantly impacts the effectiveness of deep learning algorithms.

Importance of Normalization

Normalization refers to the practice of adjusting the values of the attributes in a dataset so that they are studied within a specific range or distribute similarly. The main reason for normalizing data is to help models converge faster and more stably during the training process. Below are some specific reasons why normalization is essential:

Improved Convergence

When the input data contains features with different scales, some attributes may dominate the learning process, leading to poor model performance. For example, if we have a dataset where one feature represents height in centimeters (range 150-200) and another feature represents income in thousands of dollars (range 20-100), income will have a disproportionate weight in the cost function.

Normalizing the data brings all features to a similar scale, making it easier for optimization algorithms, such as gradient descent, to perform faster and more stable updates.

Reduced Risk of Overfitting

When we have variables with very different scales, some models may find spurious patterns that are not representative of the actual data, potentially leading to overfitting. Normalizing the data helps the model become more robust and consequently generalize better to unseen data.

Normalization Techniques

There are several normalization techniques. The most common are:

Min-Max Scaling

Min-max scaling is a simple technique that rescales features to a defined range, typically between 0 and 1. The formula to normalize a value x using this technique is:

$$x' = \frac{x - \min(X)}{\max(X) - \min(X)}$$

Where $\min(X)$ is the minimum value of the feature and $\max(X)$ is the maximum value. This technique is useful in situations where it is important to maintain the original shape of the data distribution.

Code Example

Here is an example in Python that shows how to apply min-max scaling to a dataset:

```python
import numpy as np

# Assume we have a dataset
data = np.array([150, 175, 190, 200, 160])

# Normalization using min-max scaling
data_min = data.min()
data_max = data.max()
normalized_data = (data - data_min) / (data_max - data_min)

print("Original data:", data)
print("Normalized data:", normalized_data)
```

Z-score Normalization (Standardization)

Z-score normalization, or standardization, is another technique that transforms features to have a mean of 0 and a standard deviation of 1. The formula is as follows:

$$z = \frac{x - \mu}{\sigma}$$

where μ is the mean of the feature and σ is the standard deviation. This technique is useful when the data follows a Gaussian (normal) distribution and helps reduce the impact of outliers.

Code Example

Below is an example of how to implement Z-score normalization:

```python
import numpy as np

# Dataset
data = np.array([150, 175, 190, 200, 160])

# Calculation of mean and standard deviation
mean = np.mean(data)
std_dev = np.std(data)

# Normalization using Z-score
standardized_data = (data - mean) / std_dev

print("Original data:", data)
print("Standardized data:", standardized_data)
```

Interquartile Range Normalization

Interquartile range normalization is used to scale data based on quartiles, making it robust to outliers. It is calculated using the first quartile $Q1$ and the third quartile $Q3$:

$$x' = \frac{x - Q1}{Q3 - Q1}$$

This technique is particularly useful when the data contains outliers that may distort the mean and standard deviation.

Considerations When Normalizing

When normalizing data, it's important to remember:

1. **Apply the same transformation to training and test data**: When training a model with a normalized dataset, the same transformation must be applied to the new data to ensure consistency.

2. **Store statistical information**: When applying normalization techniques that require the calculation of mean and standard deviation (or min and max), it is important to save these values for application to test data.

3. **Evaluate features**: Before deciding which normalization technique to use, it is important to explore the data and evaluate the distribution of each feature. Some techniques work better with certain types of distributions.

Conclusion

Data normalization is a critical step in preparing datasets for deep learning. By ensuring that all features contribute equally to the model's learning, convergence issues can be avoided, and the quality of the model improved. The choice of the appropriate normalization technique depends on the nature of the data and the algorithm intended for use. By mastering normalization, a solid foundation for effectively building deep learning models is established.

In the next chapter, we will explore the backpropagation algorithm, which is an essential component in training neural networks, and how it is used to adjust weights and minimize the loss function.

Backpropagation Algorithm

The backpropagation algorithm is one of the most essential and fundamental components in training neural networks. This algorithm allows a neural network to effectively adjust its weights in order to minimize the error in its predictions. In this chapter, we will explore how the backpropagation algorithm works, the logic behind it, its practical implementation, and some key intuitions about its functioning.

What is the Backpropagation Algorithm?

The backpropagation algorithm is a method used to compute the gradient of the loss function (or error) with respect to the weights of the neural network. This process is efficiently carried out by applying the chain rule of differential calculus. The main objective is to adjust the weights of the neurons based on the errors made in previous predictions, thereby enabling the network to learn to make better forecasts with each iteration.

Backpropagation Process

The backpropagation algorithm can be divided into two phases: forward propagation and backward propagation. Let's take a closer look at each of these phases.

1. Forward Propagation

In this phase, the input is sent through the neural network, layer by layer, until it reaches the output layer. In each layer, the following operations are performed:

- **Weighted Sum Calculation**: For each neuron, the input from the previous layer is multiplied by the associated weights and the bias is added:

$$z_j = \sum_i w_{ij} \cdot x_i + b_j$$

where z_j is the weighted sum for neuron j, w_{ij} are the weights, x_i are the inputs, and b_j is the bias.

- **Activation Function Application**: The weighted sum is passed through an activation function to produce the output of the neuron, introducing the necessary non-linearity into the model:

$$a_j = f(z_j)$$

where f is the applied activation function.

This process is repeated for all layers of the network until reaching the output layer, where the final prediction is made.

2. Error Calculation

Once we have obtained the output of the network, it is necessary to compare this prediction with the actual output (expected value). The loss function measures this discrepancy. For example, in classification problems, cross-entropy can be used as a loss function:

$$L(y,\hat{y}) = -\sum_i y_i \log(\hat{y}_i)$$

where y is the true label and $\hat{y}$ is the model prediction.

3. Backward Propagation

With the error calculated, the next step is to backpropagate this error through the network to update the weights. This is the heart of the backpropagation algorithm.

- **Loss Gradient Calculation**: We need to compute the derivative of the loss function with respect to each weight in the network. We use the chain rule to obtain:

$$\frac{\partial L}{\partial w_{ij}} = \frac{\partial L}{\partial a_j} \cdot \frac{\partial a_j}{\partial z_j} \cdot \frac{\partial z_j}{\partial w_{ij}}$$

This involves calculating the gradient of the error with respect to the outputs of the network and then back to the inputs, until we reach the weights.

- **Weight Update**: Once we have the gradients, we can update the weights using an optimization technique, typically gradient descent:

$$w_{ij} = w_{ij} - \eta \cdot \frac{\partial L}{\partial w_{ij}}$$

where η is the learning rate. This rate controls the magnitude of the weight update.

Backpropagation Implementation Example in Python

To illustrate how the backpropagation algorithm works, we will implement a simple neural network using NumPy. This example will use a network with one hidden layer to solve a binary classification problem.

Perceptron Implementation with Backpropagation

```python
import numpy as np

# Definition of the activation function and its derivative
def sigmoid(x):
    return 1 / (1 + np.exp(-x))

def sigmoid_derivative(x):
    return x * (1 - x)

# Example dataset (logical AND)
X = np.array([[0, 0],
              [0, 1],
              [1, 0],
              [1, 1]])
y = np.array([[0],
              [0],
              [0],
              [1]])

# Weight initialization
np.random.seed(42)  # For reproducibility
weights_input_hidden = np.random.uniform(size=(2, 2))
```

```python
    # 2 inputs to 2 hidden neurons
23  weights_hidden_output = np.random.uniform(size=(2, 1))
    # 2 hidden neurons to 1 output
24
25  # Parameters
26  learning_rate = 0.5
27  epochs = 10000
28
29  # Training the neural network
30  for epoch in range(epochs):
31      # Forward propagation
32      hidden_layer_input = np.dot(X, weights_input_hidden)
33      hidden_layer_output = sigmoid(hidden_layer_input)
34
35      output_layer_input = np.dot(hidden_layer_output,
    weights_hidden_output)
36      predicted_output = sigmoid(output_layer_input)
37
38      # Error calculation
39      error = y - predicted_output
40
41      # Backpropagation
42      d_predicted_output = error * sigmoid_derivative(
    predicted_output)
43      error_hidden_layer = d_predicted_output.dot(
    weights_hidden_output.T)
44      d_hidden_layer = error_hidden_layer *
    sigmoid_derivative(hidden_layer_output)
45
46      # Weight update
47      weights_hidden_output += hidden_layer_output.T.dot(
    d_predicted_output) * learning_rate
48      weights_input_hidden += X.T.dot(d_hidden_layer) *
    learning_rate
49
```

```
50  # Final predictions
51  print("Predictions after training:")
52  print(predicted_output)
```

Code Breakdown

1. **Definition of Functions**: The sigmoid activation function and its derivative are defined. These functions will be used for both forward propagation and backpropagation.

2. **Dataset**: The logical AND dataset is used, which is a simple binary problem.

3. **Weight Initialization**: Weights are initialized randomly. The dimensions are based on the network architecture.

4. **Training**: In each epoch:

   - Forward propagation is performed to obtain predictions.

   - The error between predictions and actual outputs is calculated.

   - Backpropagation is conducted to compute the gradients.

   - Weights are updated using the learning rate.

5. **Final Predictions**: After the entire training process, the resultant predictions of the network are printed.

Importance of the Backpropagation Algorithm

The backpropagation algorithm is fundamental in the development of deep learning models because it enables neural networks to adapt to data and learn complex patterns. Here are some key reasons why it is important:

- **Efficiency**: It calculates gradients efficiently using the chain rule. This allows networks to be deeper and more complex without a significant increase in computation time.

- **Flexibility**: It can be used with nearly any neural network architecture and adapts to multiple loss functions, making it versatile.

- **Advancement in AI**: Backpropagation has enabled the development of advanced models in fields such as computer vision and natural language processing, greatly expanding the capabilities of artificial intelligence.

Conclusions

The backpropagation algorithm is a crucial element in training neural networks, allowing the model to learn from its errors and adapt to make more accurate predictions. By understanding its functioning and implementation, a solid foundation is laid for building and optimizing artificial intelligence models in various applications. As we progress through this book, we will delve into other techniques and algorithms that complement and enhance the use of neural networks in deep learning.

Gradient Descent Methods

Gradient descent is one of the most commonly used algorithms in the training of machine learning models, particularly in neural networks. Its main function is to minimize the loss function, which measures how well the model performs compared to the actual values. In this chapter, we will explore how gradient descent works, the most common variants, and how they are used in the context of deep learning.

What is Gradient Descent?

Gradient descent is an iterative algorithm used to find the optimal values of the model parameters (weights and biases). The basic idea is to update the parameters in the opposite direction of the gradient of the loss function with respect to those parameters. This occurs by seeking the direction of greatest descent, which translates into a reduction of the loss function.

Visualizing Gradient Descent: Imagine standing at the top of a mountain and wanting to get down to the nearest valley. Gradient descent would be like looking down around you and choosing the steepest direction to descend. With each step you take, you recalculate the slope to ensure you're always going downhill.

The Gradient Descent Formula

Mathematically, the parameter update can be described as:

$$\theta := \theta - \eta \cdot \nabla J(\theta)$$

where:

- θ represents the model parameters (weights and biases).
- η is the learning rate, a hyperparameter that controls the size of each step we take towards the minimum.
- $\nabla J(\theta)$ is the gradient of the loss function J with respect to θ.

Types of Gradient Descent

There are several variants of gradient descent, each with its advantages and disadvantages. The most common are:

Batch Gradient Descent

In batch gradient descent, all training data is used to compute the gradient before updating the parameters. This approach ensures that the descent direction is accurate, but it can be computationally expensive and slow, especially with large datasets.

- **Advantages**:
    - Provides an accurate estimate of the gradient as it is

based on the entire dataset.

- ◦ Converges towards the global minimum in convex problems, meaning it can find the best possible solution.

- **Disadvantages**:

  - ◦ Can be very slow, as it needs to process the entire dataset before updating the weights.

  - ◦ Requires a lot of computational space to store all the data, which can be a problem in large applications.

Stochastic Gradient Descent (SGD)

Stochastic gradient descent updates the parameters after calculating the gradient using only a random sample from the dataset in each iteration. This makes the optimization process faster and more efficient, although it may introduce some noise into the convergence process.

- **Advantages**:

  - ◦ Much faster than batch gradient descent, making it convenient for very large datasets.

  - ◦ The randomness can help the model escape local minima as it can better explore the cost surface.

- **Disadvantages**:

  - ◦ The gradient direction can be noisy, which can cause oscillations and make the convergence process more erratic.

  - ◦ It may not converge effectively if the learning rate is too high.

Mini-batch Gradient Descent

Mini-batch gradient descent combines the advantages of both batch and stochastic gradient descent. Instead of using the entire dataset or a single sample, a small subset of data (mini-batch) is taken to calculate the gradient and update the parameters.

- **Advantages**:

    - Fast and efficient, balancing accuracy and computational cost. It allows leveraging the full processing capability of GPUs.

    - Less noise in the gradient update than stochastic SGD, which allows for more stable convergence.

- **Disadvantages**:

    - The choice of mini-batch size can affect performance and convergence. A size that is too small can introduce noise, while one that is too large can be similar to the full batch.

Learning Rate

The learning rate η is a critical hyperparameter in training. It controls the magnitude of the parameter updates and can significantly impact the convergence of the algorithm. Choosing a learning rate that is too high can cause the model to diverge, while a rate that is too low can make the training process extremely slow.

Learning Rate Scheduling

A common technique is learning rate scheduling, where the learning rate is gradually decreased as training progresses. This strategy, known as "learning rate decay," allows the model to take large steps initially and then approach the minimum more precisely towards the end of the process.

Variants of Gradient Descent

In addition to the choice between SGD and batch gradient descent, there are variants that have proven effective in practice:

Momentum

The Momentum method accelerates gradient descent by adding a fraction of the previous gradient to the current update. This allows the model to "speed up" in directions where it has had a consistent gradient.

The update is performed as follows:

$$v_t = \beta v_{t-1} + (1 - \beta)\nabla J(\theta) \quad \theta := \theta - \eta v_t$$

where v_t is the velocity, and β is a hyperparameter that controls the amount of momentum applied. This method helps to smooth the updates and can aid in overcoming oscillations on the cost surface.

Adam (Adaptive Moment Estimation)

Adam is one of the most popular optimization methods due to its efficiency and adaptability. It combines the ideas of Momentum and adaptive learning rate adjustment. Adam maintains an estimate of the first moment (the average of the gradients) and the second moment (the variance of the gradients).

Updates are performed as follows:

$$v_t = \beta_1 v_{t-1} + (1 - \beta_1)\nabla J(\theta) \ s_t = \beta_2 s_{t-1} + (1 - \beta_2)(\nabla J(\theta))^2$$

The weights are updated as:

$$\theta := \theta - \frac{\eta v_t}{\sqrt{s_t} + \diamondsuit}$$

where $\diamondsuit$ is a small number to prevent division by zero. This method is particularly effective for mini-batches and can adapt efficiently to different parameters, making adjustments based on the gradient history.

Implementation Example in Python

Below is a practical example illustrating how to implement gradient descent using stochastic gradient descent in a simple linear regression problem. We will use Python and the `NumPy` library.

```python
import numpy as np

# Generating synthetic data
np.random.seed(42)
X = 2 * np.random.rand(100, 1)
y = 4 + 3 * X + np.random.randn(100, 1)

# Parameters initialization
theta = np.random.randn(2, 1)   # Initial weights
learning_rate = 0.1
n_iterations = 1000
m = len(y)

```

```
14   X_b = np.c_[np.ones((m, 1)), X]  # adding the intercept
15
16   # Gradient descent implementation
17   for iteration in range(n_iterations):
18       gradients = 2/m * X_b.T.dot(X_b.dot(theta) - y)
     # gradient calculation
19       theta -= learning_rate * gradients
     # updating the parameters
20
21   print("Optimal weights:", theta)
```

In this example, we generated synthetic data for a simple linear regression problem. Then, we randomly initialized the parameters (weights) and applied gradient descent to optimize them. At the end, we print the optimized weights.

Conclusions

Gradient descent is a fundamental technique in the world of deep learning and machine learning. Its different variants, including batch gradient descent, stochastic gradient descent, and mini-batch gradient descent, offer options that adapt to various situations and datasets. Understanding these methods, along with the correct choice of learning rates and the implementation of techniques like Momentum and Adam, can mean the difference between a model that successfully converges and one that does not.

As we progress through the following chapters, we will explore additional techniques that further optimize the training process of neural networks and strategies to address specific issues in training deep learning models.

Introduction to Convolutional Neural Networks

Convolutional Neural Networks (CNNs) are a specialized neural network architecture designed to process data with a grid-like structure, such as images. Over the last decade, they have revolutionized the field of computer vision by providing effective solutions for tasks like image classification, object detection, and semantic segmentation. In this chapter, we will explore the fundamental concepts behind convolutional networks, their architecture, and how they can be applied to real-world problems.

What are Convolutional Neural Networks?

Convolutional Neural Networks are inspired by the structure of the human brain, where neurons are organized in layers that process different aspects of incoming information. In the case of CNNs, the primary functionality is to extract hierarchical features from images through a convolutional process, enabling the network to learn complex and relevant patterns efficiently.

Unlike fully connected neural networks, where each neuron is connected to all neurons in the previous layer, CNNs use filters (or kernels) that slide (or convolve) over the input. This approach allows CNNs to be more efficient in terms of parameters and computation by focusing on the local features of the data.

Structure of a Convolutional Network

A typical CNN consists of several layers that perform specific roles. Although there can be many variations in architecture, the following layers are fundamental in most CNNs:

Convolutional Layer

The convolutional layer is the heart of the convolutional network. Here, one or more filters are applied to the input. Each filter is a small matrix that scans the image (or input volume) and performs the convolution operation, which can be mathematically defined as:

$$(S * K)(i,j) = \sum_m \sum_n S(m, n)K(i - m, j - n)$$

where S is the input, K is the filter, and (i,j) represents the position where the filter is applied.

The result of the convolution is called the feature map or activation. This process allows the network to detect features such as edges, textures, and patterns in the image.

Activation Layer

After the convolutional layer, an activation function is applied. The ReLU (Rectified Linear Unit) function is the most commonly used, as it introduces non-linearities into the model, allowing CNNs to learn more complex patterns. The ReLU function is defined as:

$$f(x) = \max(0, x)$$

This function "activates" positive values and converts negative values to zero, which is useful for avoiding the vanishing gradient problem.

Pooling Layer

The pooling layer is used to reduce the dimensions of the feature map, helping to decrease the number of parameters and thus avoid overfitting. The most common pooling method is max pooling, which takes the maximum value in a specific window of the input. Mathematically, this can be expressed as:

$$Y(i,j) = \max_{m,n} X(m, n)$$

where Y is the result of the max pooling over the input window X. This dimensionality reduction process allows the network to be more manageable and to focus on the most important features.

Fully Connected Layers

At the end of a convolutional network, the extracted features are passed through one or more fully connected (FC) layers. These layers function like a traditional neural network, where each neuron is connected to all neurons in the previous layer. This setup allows for classification or regression based on the features learned during previous stages. The final output of the network can be processed through a layer with a softmax activation function for multi-class classification tasks.

Training Process of a Convolutional Network

The training process of a convolutional network is similar to that of other neural network architectures, involving two phases: forward propagation and backpropagation.

Forward Propagation

1. **Convolution**: The feature map activations are calculated by applying convolution filters to the input.

2. **Activation**: An activation function such as ReLU is applied to the calculated activations.

3. **Pooling**: Dimensionality is reduced through a pooling layer.

4. **Forward propagation through fully connected layers**: The extracted features are used for classification or regression.

Backpropagation

In backpropagation, the gradient of the loss function with respect to the network's weights is calculated, and these weights are updated using an optimization method such as gradient descent. The process includes:

1. **Error Calculation**: The predicted output is compared with the ground truth using a loss function.

2. **Gradient Calculation**: The gradient of the error with respect to the previous layers is calculated using the chain rule.

3. **Weight Update**: Weights are adjusted to minimize the loss function.

Example Implementation of a CNN in Python

Let's look at a simple example using Keras, a high-level library for building and training neural networks in Python. In this case, we will create a CNN to classify images from the CIFAR-10 dataset, which contains 60,000 images across 10 different classes.

```python
import numpy as np
import tensorflow as tf
from tensorflow.keras import layers, models
from tensorflow.keras.datasets import cifar10

# Load the CIFAR-10 dataset
(X_train, y_train), (X_test, y_test) = cifar10.load_data()

# Normalize the data
X_train = X_train.astype('float32') / 255.0
X_test = X_test.astype('float32') / 255.0

# Convert labels to categorical format
y_train = tf.keras.utils.to_categorical(y_train, 10)
y_test = tf.keras.utils.to_categorical(y_test, 10)

# Create the convolutional neural network model
model = models.Sequential()

# Convolutional Layer 1
model.add(layers.Conv2D(32, (3, 3), activation='relu',
    input_shape=(32, 32, 3)))
model.add(layers.MaxPooling2D((2, 2)))

# Convolutional Layer 2
```

```
25  model.add(layers.Conv2D(64, (3, 3), activation='relu'))
26  model.add(layers.MaxPooling2D((2, 2)))
27
28  # Convolutional Layer 3
29  model.add(layers.Conv2D(64, (3, 3), activation='relu'))
30
31  # Flatten the activations
32  model.add(layers.Flatten())
33  model.add(layers.Dense(64, activation='relu'))
34
35  # Output Layer
36  model.add(layers.Dense(10, activation='softmax'))
37
38  # Compile the model
39  model.compile(optimizer='adam',
40                loss='categorical_crossentropy',
41                metrics=['accuracy'])
42
43  # Train the model
44  model.fit(X_train, y_train, epochs=10, batch_size=64,
    validation_data=(X_test, y_test))
45
46  # Evaluate the model
47  test_loss, test_acc = model.evaluate(X_test, y_test)
48  print(f'Test accuracy: {test_acc}')
```

Code Details

1. **Loading and Preparing Data**: We load the CIFAR-10 dataset and normalize the pixel values to the range [0, 1]. We also convert the labels into one-hot encoded format for training.

2. **Building the CNN**: We define a series of convolutional layers followed by pooling layers, and finally dense layers for

classification. Each convolutional layer uses ReLU activation, and the output layer uses softmax activation to classify images into 10 different classes.

3. **Compiling and Training**: We compile the model using the Adam optimizer and cross-entropy loss function. Then, the model is trained on the dataset for 10 epochs.

4. **Evaluating the Model**: Finally, we evaluate the model's performance on the test set.

Applications of Convolutional Neural Networks

Convolutional neural networks have a wide range of applications in the real world:

- **Image Classification**: The most common task, where models are trained to classify images into different categories (e.g., cat vs. dog).

- **Object Detection**: Used in surveillance systems and autonomous vehicles to identify and locate objects in real-time.

- **Image Segmentation**: Pixel-wise classification, such as in medical applications to identify tumors in MRI images.

- **Character Recognition**: Used in OCR (Optical Character Recognition) technologies to extract text from images.

Final Considerations

Convolutional neural networks have significantly changed the landscape of deep learning and computer vision. Their ability to automatically learn the relevant features of the data makes them a powerful tool for solving a variety of complex tasks. As we continue to advance in this book, we will explore more advanced techniques and architectures and their applications to various real-world problems, delving into how CNNs are poised to tackle the challenges of the future in artificial intelligence.

In the next chapter, we will explore convolution operations in more depth, as well as optimization techniques and activation visualization in convolutional networks.

## Chapter 13

Convolution Operations

Convolution operations are the core of convolutional neural networks (CNNs), which have proven to be especially effective in image processing and pattern recognition tasks. Convolution is a mathematical operation that allows the combination of two functions to produce a third one. In the context of CNNs, it is used to extract features from the input data by applying filters (or kernels). In this chapter, we will explore in depth what convolution is, how it is performed, its properties, and the different ways to apply it in the context of neural networks.

What is Convolution?

Convolution in the realm of deep learning involves applying a filter or kernel over an input, producing a feature map that captures relevant information about the original input. This process enables the network to detect patterns, textures, edges, and other elements of interest in the data.

Mathematically, the convolution operation between an image I and a filter K can be expressed as:

$$S(i,j) = \sum_m \sum_n I(m, n)K(i - m, j - n)$$

where S is the result of the convolution, I is the input image, K is the kernel, and (i, j) are the output coordinates.

Convolution Process

The convolution process involves several stages:

1. **Filter Definition**: A filter or kernel is chosen, which is a small matrix (for example, 3x3) used to extract features. The values of the filter are parameters that are learned during training.

2. **Filter Sliding**: The filter slides over the input image, performing the convolution operation for each position. The result at each position is stored in a feature map.

3. **Feature Map Calculation**: At each position, the weighted sum of the image values contained within the area covered by the filter is calculated. This presents how the filter has captured local information in the image.

Visualization of the Process

Imagine we have a 5x5 pixel image and a 3x3 filter. The convolution would be performed as follows:

- In the first step, the filter overlaps the top left corner of the image. Then, the resulting value is calculated by performing the sum of products, where each filter value multiplies the corresponding value in the image.

- After calculating this value, the filter moves one position to the right or downward (depending on the stride), and the process is repeated until the entire image is covered.

Stride and Padding

Stride

Stride refers to how many positions the filter moves in each operation. By default, the stride is 1, but other values can be applied to alter the size of the computed feature map. A larger stride results in a smaller feature map, while a smaller stride produces a wider map.

Padding

Padding is a technique used to control the size of the resulting feature map. It involves adding zeros around the edges of the input image. This is useful for preserving the spatial dimension of the input. There are different types of padding:

- **Valid Padding**: No padding is added to the image, so the size of the feature map is smaller than that of the input.

- **Same Padding**: Zeros are added in such a way that the size of the feature map is the same as that of the input.

Example of Convolution in Python

Let's implement a basic convolution operation in Python using `NumPy` to illustrate how it works.

```
1   import numpy as np
```

```python
2
3   # Definition of an input image (5x5)
4   image = np.array([[1, 2, 3, 0, 1],
5                     [0, 1, 2, 3, 0],
6                     [1, 2, 0, 1, 1],
7                     [0, 3, 2, 0, 0],
8                     [1, 0, 1, 2, 3]])
9
10  # Definition of the filter (3x3)
11  kernel = np.array([[1, 0, -1],
12                     [1, 0, -1],
13                     [1, 0, -1]])
14
15  # Dimensions of the image and the filter
16  image_height, image_width = image.shape
17  kernel_height, kernel_width = kernel.shape
18
19  # Calculate the dimension of the feature map
20  output_height = image_height - kernel_height + 1
21  output_width = image_width - kernel_width + 1
22
23  # Create the feature map
24  output = np.zeros((output_height, output_width))
25
26  # Apply the convolution
27  for i in range(output_height):
28      for j in range(output_width):
29          # Multiplication and sum of products
30          output[i, j] = np.sum(image[i:i + kernel_height, j:
    j + kernel_width] * kernel)
31
32  print("Feature map:")
33  print(output)
```

Explanation of the Code

1. **Definition of the Image and the Filter**: A 5x5 image and a 3x3 filter are defined.

2. **Dimension Calculation**: The dimensions of the resulting feature map are determined by subtracting the size of the filter from the size of the image.

3. **Convolution Application**: All valid positions of the image are traversed, and the dot product between the area covered by the filter and the filter itself is calculated.

4. **Results**: The resulting values are stored in the feature map and printed.

Differences Between Convolution and Correlation

It is crucial to distinguish between the convolution operation and that of correlation. Although they are often used interchangeably in the context of deep learning, the mathematical connotation is different. Convolution involves rotating the filter 180 degrees before applying it:

$$S(i,j) = (I * K)(i,j) = \sum_m \sum_n I(i+m, j+n) K(-m, -n)$$

However, in many practical implementations, especially in the context of CNNs, the rotation of the filter is not always applied, which can lead to confusion.

Applications of Convolution

Convolution operations are fundamental in several applications:

- **Computer Vision**: Edge detection, texture analysis, and pattern recognition in images.

- **Image Recognition**: Image classification and object detection using convolutional networks.

- **Image Filtering**: Improving image quality and removing noise.

- **Signal Processing**: Applications in audio and signaling, where filters are used to extract relevant components.

Conclusions

Convolution operations are a powerful technique in the field of deep learning, especially within convolutional neural networks. By allowing hierarchical feature extraction from data, convolution enables networks to identify complex patterns. Understanding the concepts of convolution, stride, and padding is fundamental for designing effective models that address computer vision problems and other domains. As we delve deeper into convolutional networks, we will explore advanced concepts and architectures that evolve on the basis of these fundamental operations.

Fundamentals of Recurrent Networks

Recurrent Neural Networks (RNNs) are a special class of neural networks designed to process sequential data. Unlike traditional neural networks, where the inputs are independent of each other, RNNs can retain information from previous inputs and use it to influence the current output. This approach makes them a powerful tool for a wide range of applications, including natural language processing, time series analysis, and much more. The ability to learn from temporal sequences makes RNNs ideal for modeling data where order and context are crucial.

What are Recurrent Neural Networks?

RNNs are designed to work with sequences of data, which can range from a series of timesteps in financial analysis to a sequence of words in a text. The design of RNNs includes a "memory" mechanism that allows them to maintain and utilize past information as sequences flow through the network. This not only enhances context understanding but also improves their ability to predict future outcomes based on previously observed patterns. This feature is essential in tasks where temporal dependency and context are fundamental, making them significantly more advanced than traditional neural networks, which typically handle inputs in isolation.

Architecture of an RNN

The basic structure of an RNN includes several fundamental components. The input consists of a sequence of data, which could be a vector representing significant aspects at each moment. For example, in a natural language processing context, each word can be represented as a vector in a vector space that captures its meaning and semantic relationships.

The "hidden state" of the network encapsulates information from previous inputs and is updated at each timestep to retain and process key information from the sequence. This hidden state acts as the medium through which the network remembers its history and uses it to inform its current decisions.

Additionally, it is important to mention that the RNN can produce output at each timestep, which is determined by both the current input and the hidden state that has evolved throughout the sequence. This structure allows the network to make dynamic and contextual predictions, which is crucial in applications where the sequence of data affects the outcome.

Visualizing the Hidden State

If we visualize the flow of information in an RNN, we can imagine that each node in the network acts as a small processor that takes as input not only the present data but also information derived from history. In this sense, the cyclic connection between the hidden states allows the model to capture temporal dependencies, making it extremely effective for classification and prediction problems that require this capability.

Calculating the Hidden State

Mathematically, the hidden state h_t in an RNN is updated using a formula that combines information from the previous hidden state and the current input. Specifically:

$$h_t = f(W_h h_{t-1} + W_x x_t + b)$$

In this equation, W_h are the weights connecting the previous hidden state to the current state, and W_x are the weights connecting the current input to the hidden state. The bias b and the activation function f, which is usually a non-linear function like hyperbolic tangent or ReLU, complete the RNN mechanism.

Output of the RNN

The output y_t generated by the RNN is calculated from the hidden state as follows:

$$y_t = g(W_y h_t + b_y)$$

Where W_y are the weights associated with the network's output and g can be an appropriate activation function, such as softmax for classification tasks or sigmoid for regression.

Common Problems in RNNs

Despite their power, RNNs face several significant challenges. One of the most notable is the *vanishing gradient* problem. This phenomenon occurs when an RNN is trained on long sequences, where the gradients that propagate through time tend to become extremely small. As a result, it becomes difficult to learn long-term relationships, limiting the effectiveness of learning.

Vanishing and Exploding Gradients

The vanishing gradient problem implies that gradients decrease exponentially as they propagate back through the layers of the network. This effect is particularly problematic for networks that have many layers or require remembering information across long sequences. Additionally, there is the opposite phenomenon known as *exploding gradients*, which refers to an extreme increase in gradient values, which can cause weights to update unstably and ultimately cause the model to diverge completely.

Applications of RNNs

RNNs have proven to be highly effective in a variety of applications, particularly where ordering and temporality are essential. First, in natural language processing (NLP), RNNs are foundational for tasks such as machine translation, where understanding context and temporal dependencies between words is crucial. For example, in translating a sentence, the meaning of a word may depend on its relationship to other words in the sentence.

RNNs are also very useful in time series analysis, where they can be applied in forecasting financial data or performance metrics over time. Using past patterns, RNNs can predict future stock prices or sales trends, thus facilitating strategic decision-making in business.

Additionally, they generate text automatically, which is exciting in content creation or chatbots. These models can learn to construct coherent and contextual sentences based on an initial topic or a set of words. This allows machines to understand and generate language in a more human-like manner.

More innovatively, RNNs have begun to be utilized in generative music systems and voice synthesis, where they can learn from large audio databases, understanding the structure and rhythm of music or the natural flow of speech to create new compositions or vocal responses.

Long Short-Term Memory (LSTM)

To address the vanishing and exploding gradient problems that arise in conventional RNNs, Long Short-Term Memory (LSTM) networks were developed. These networks include memory cells that allow the network to retain information over extended periods, making them especially effective for tasks where data at different points in the sequence is interconnected over time.

LSTMs differ from standard RNNs in their unique architecture, which includes three "gates" that control the flow of information. Each of these gates has a crucial role:

First, the **forget gate**, which determines what information from the previous memory state should be forgotten. This is an essential feature because it allows the network to discard irrelevant information, ensuring that only data that truly matters influences future decisions.

Second, the **input gate**, which controls what new information will be stored in the current memory state. This enables the network to learn from new inputs and retain significant data in the memory cell.

Finally, the **output gate** decides what information from the memory state should be used as output at that specific moment. This allows the network to use only the information that is relevant and useful for the current prediction.

These components, and the way they interact, allow LSTMs to effectively learn long-term dependencies, overcoming the vanishing gradient problem that hindered traditional RNNs. In situations where there is much dependency between distant events, using LSTMs is highly beneficial, as they can remember key information across extensive data chains.

Gated Recurrent Unit (GRU)

Another innovative variant of RNNs is the Gated Recurrent Unit (GRU), which simplifies the architecture of LSTMs by combining the input and forget gates into a single update gate. This design not only enhances efficiency in terms of memory and computation but also allows the GRU to maintain performance comparable to LSTMs on many tasks.

Like LSTMs, GRUs have two main gates: the **update gate**, which controls what information from the previous state should be retained and how much new information should be incorporated, and the **reset gate**, which determines how much of the previous information should be ignored. This simplification in structure, by merging the control of inputs and forgets, allows GRUs to be faster to train and less prone to overfitting issues.

The GRU is especially useful in cases where smaller datasets are available, or quick implementation solutions are needed, as its lower complexity in architecture generally translates to shorter training times without significantly sacrificing output quality. The choice between using an LSTM or a GRU often depends on the specific problem at hand, the amount of data available for training, and the developer's preferences, as both architectures are effective in their respective domains.

Example of RNN Implementation in Python

To illustrate how to implement a simple RNN, we will use Keras, a high-level library for building and training deep learning models. We will address a practical case where we generate text from word sequences.

```
1   import numpy as np
2   import tensorflow as tf
3   from tensorflow.keras import layers, models
```

```python
4
5  # Generating a synthetic dataset
6  text =
   "Hello, these are some example sentences that we are going
   to use in our RNN."

7  corpus = text.lower().split()
8  word_to_index = {word: i for i, word in enumerate(set(
   corpus))}
9  index_to_word = {i: word for word, i in word_to_index.items
   ()}
10
11 # Creating input and output sequences
12 sequence_length = 3
13 X = []
14 y = []
15
16 for i in range(len(corpus) - sequence_length):
17     X.append([word_to_index[corpus[i + j]] for j in range(
   sequence_length)])
18     y.append(word_to_index[corpus[i + sequence_length]])
19
20 X = np.array(X)
21 y = np.array(y)
22
23 # Defining the RNN model
24 model = models.Sequential()
25 model.add(layers.Embedding(input_dim=len(word_to_index),
      output_dim=10, input_length=sequence_length))
26 model.add(layers.SimpleRNN(10))
   # RNN layer with 10 neurons
27 model.add(layers.Dense(len(word_to_index), activation=
   'softmax'))  # Output layer
28
29 # Compiling the model
```

```
30  model.compile(loss='sparse_categorical_crossentropy',
    optimizer='adam', metrics=['accuracy'])
31
32  # Training the model
33  model.fit(X, y, epochs=100, verbose=0)
34
35  # Making a prediction
36  test_sequence = [word_to_index[word] for word in ["are",
    "some", "example"]]
37  predicted_word_index = np.argmax(model.predict(np.array([
    test_sequence])))
38  predicted_word = index_to_word[predicted_word_index]
39
40  print(f"The predicted word for the sequence is: '{
    predicted_word}'")
```

Code Details

We start by generating a synthetic dataset, taking a simple text and processing it into sequences. Indices are assigned to each word, and from there, the necessary input and output sequences are created for training the network.

We create a basic RNN model that includes an embedding layer to represent each word in the sequence and an RNN layer that handles processing and making predictions. The architecture culminates in a dense layer that uses the softmax activation function, which is suitable for classification tasks.

Once the model has been compiled and trained, a prediction is made on a word sequence, demonstrating how the RNN can generate results based on the provided context.

Conclusions

Recurrent neural networks are a fundamental pillar in deep learning, particularly in handling sequential data. Although traditional RNNs face significant challenges like the vanishing gradient problem, their modern variants like LSTM and GRU have proven to be highly effective, allowing models to learn and retain information over extended periods.

With applications ranging from natural language processing to time series prediction, the relevance of RNNs extends across multiple fields, making them vital tools for advancement and innovation in artificial intelligence technology. Ongoing exploration in this area suggests that RNNs will continue to be an active domain for research, development, and application in the future.

Long Short-Term Memory (LSTM)

Long Short-Term Memory networks, commonly known as LSTM, represent one of the most significant evolutions in the field of deep learning. These networks were developed to address the inherent problems of traditional Recurrent Neural Networks (RNN), particularly concerning gradient vanishing, a crucial challenge when working with long data sequences. The unique structure and advanced architecture of LSTMs allow them not only to learn short-term patterns but also to establish meaningful long-term connections, making them an essential tool for complex tasks in natural language processing and other domains where sequence and context are vital.

LSTM Architecture

Unlike standard RNNs, which have a relatively simple structure, the architecture of an LSTM is richer and more sophisticated. This additional complexity is necessary for the network to effectively manage information through its various processing phases. At the heart of an LSTM are the fundamental components: memory cells, gates, and hidden states. But what do these terms imply, and how do they work in harmony?

Key Components of an LSTM

First, the memory cells are the functional core of the LSTM. These cells act as a storage system that allows the network to remember important information over time. Unlike traditional RNNs, which can forget critical information as it propagates, the memory cells of LSTMs are designed to retain valuable data over extended periods, making them ideal for tasks where previous information is essential. For example, when translating a sentence, understanding the meaning of a word may depend on the words that precede it in the same sentence.

LSTMs have three types of gates that control the flow of information to and from these memory cells. These gates function as switches that can be open or closed based on the information they receive. The first gate is the **forget gate**, which decides what information from the previous memory cell should be discarded. This forgetting mechanism is crucial; it allows the network not to cling to irrelevant information, consequently resolving the vanishing gradient issue. For example, if a word in a sentence does not affect the meaning of subsequent words, the forget gate may allow it to be discarded.

Secondly, the **input gate** regulates what new information can be added to the memory cell. This component ensures that the network stores data that is useful for future computations. Thus, the input gate allows relevant information to be efficiently integrated, helping the network build a solid knowledge base.

Finally, the **output gate** determines what information from the memory cell will be used to calculate the output at the current time. Similar to a reception desk that decides what information to provide to visitors, the output gate filters and delivers only the essential information.

Calculations in an LSTM

The wonder of LSTMs lies in how they integrate these components through precise calculations. The update of the internal state of the LSTM, as well as the production of outputs, can be mathematically described. For the calculation of the forget gate, a sigmoid function is used to generate a value between 0 and 1, where a value of 0 means "forget everything" and 1 means "remember everything." Mathematically, this is expressed as:

$$f_t = \sigma(W_f \cdot [h_{t-1}, x_t] + b_f)$$

In this expression, h_{t-1} represents the previous hidden state and x_t is the current input. The weights W_f are parameters of the network to be learned during training, and b_f is a bias used to facilitate model adjustment.

Continuing, the input gate also uses a sigmoid function and is complemented by the calculation of a new candidate state obtained through the hyperbolic tangent function:

$$i_t = \sigma(W_i \cdot [h_{t-1}, x_t] + b_i) \quad \tilde{C}_t = \tanh(W_C \cdot [h_{t-1}, x_t] + b_C)$$

The new memory state C_t is calculated by combining the information that is retained and the new information that is integrated, ensuring that the memory cell is updated effectively:

$$C_t = f_t \cdot C_{t-1} + i_t \cdot \tilde{C}_t$$

Finally, the hidden state h_t is calculated using the output gate and the updated memory state:

$$o_t = \sigma(W_o \cdot [h_{t-1}, x_t] + b_o) \quad h_t = o_t \cdot \tanh(C_t)$$

This mathematical framework not only allows for the flow of information but also highlights the elegance of LSTMs in managing relationships that extend across input sequences.

Advantages of LSTMs

LSTMs have gained popularity in the realm of deep learning thanks to their multiple advantages. Among them, the ability to handle long-term dependencies is crucial. This means that LSTMs can remember and use information from previous time steps to influence the current output. In the context of machine translation, this capability is vital. When translating a sentence, the meaning of a word may depend on several earlier words, necessitating that the network keep track of the entire context.

Additionally, by avoiding gradient vanishing, LSTMs enable more effective training compared to traditional RNNs. This structured solution that the use of gates provides allows for fine-tuning in how networks process information, leading to a more robust learning capability.

The flexibility of LSTMs is another notable advantage, as they can be applied to various types of data. Whether it is text, time sequences in financial data, or even audio, LSTMs are capable of adapting to different contexts, opening a wide range of possibilities in multiple applications.

Applications of LSTMs

The applications of LSTMs are vast and varied, spanning multiple areas of artificial intelligence. In natural language processing (NLP), these networks are extremely valuable. For example, when translating a sentence into another language, the LSTM can maintain the context of the words, ensuring that translations are accurate and contextually relevant. Moreover, in text generation, LSTMs can construct sentences, paragraphs, and even complete articles, mimicking the style and tone of a given author. This has revolutionized how machines interact with human language, enabling the creation of advanced chatbots that can communicate coherently and fluently.

Another area where LSTMs find significant use is in time series analysis. In finance, for instance, they are applied to predict future market behaviors based on historical patterns. This includes predicting stock prices, analyzing cryptocurrency prices, and identifying trends in sales data. LSTMs become crucial tools for analysts looking to make informed decisions based on accurate forecasts.

Speech recognition also greatly benefits from the use of LSTMs. Since speech is inherently sequential, with the pronunciation of words influencing how context is understood, LSTMs allow for the processing of these audio sequences and providing accurate transcriptions. By capturing patterns and correlations in voice data, these networks can convert human speech into text, facilitating interaction between humans and machines.

LSTM Implementation Example in Python

To illustrate how the power of LSTMs can be applied in real-world situations, we will implement an LSTM model using Keras to predict the next word in a simple text sequence. This example highlights not only the simplicity of building an LSTM model but also the effectiveness of these networks in capturing contextual patterns through sequences.

Setting Up the Environment

First, make sure to have the required packages installed:

```
1  pip install numpy tensorflow
```

Implementation Code

```python
1   import numpy as np
2   import tensorflow as tf
3   from tensorflow.keras import layers, models
4
5   # Generating a synthetic dataset
6   text =
    "Hello, these are some example sentences that we are going
    to use in our LSTM."

7   corpus = text.lower().split()
8   word_to_index = {word: i for i, word in enumerate(set(
    corpus))}
9   index_to_word = {i: word for word, i in word_to_index.items
    ()}
10
11  # Creating input and output sequences
12  sequence_length = 3
13  X = []
14  y = []
15
16  for i in range(len(corpus) - sequence_length):
17      X.append([word_to_index[corpus[i + j]] for j in range(
        sequence_length)])
18      y.append(word_to_index[corpus[i + sequence_length]])
19
20  X = np.array(X)
21  y = np.array(y)
22
23  # Defining the LSTM model
24  model = models.Sequential()
25  model.add(layers.Embedding(input_dim=len(word_to_index),
        output_dim=10, input_length=sequence_length))
```

```
26  model.add(layers.LSTM(10))  # LSTM layer with 10 units
27  model.add(layers.Dense(len(word_to_index), activation=
    'softmax'))  # Output layer
28
29  # Compiling the model
30  model.compile(loss='sparse_categorical_crossentropy',
    optimizer='adam', metrics=['accuracy'])
31
32  # Training the model
33  model.fit(X, y, epochs=100, verbose=0)
34
35  # Making a prediction
36  test_sequence = [word_to_index[word] for word in ["are",
    "some", "example"]]
37  predicted_word_index = np.argmax(model.predict(np.array([
    test_sequence])))
38  predicted_word = index_to_word[predicted_word_index]
39
40  print(f"The predicted word for the sequence is: '{
    predicted_word}'")
```

Code Details

1. **Data Generation**: We create a simple corpus, breaking it down into a set of input and output sequences. This ensures that the network understands the contextual relationship of the words.

2. **Model Design**: We create a model that incorporates an embedding layer to convert words into dense vectors and an LSTM layer to capture the temporality in the sequences. The output is generated through a dense layer that applies softmax to produce probabilities.

3. **Training**: We then compile and train the model using cross-

entropy loss as a loss function, with the Adam optimizer, which is effective for complex optimization problems.

4. **Prediction**: Finally, we run a prediction on a test sequence, exemplifying how the LSTM uses its prior knowledge to predict the next word in the sequence.

Conclusions

LSTMs are undoubtedly a powerhouse in the realm of deep learning, providing robust solutions for handling sequential data. Their innovative nature allows them to remember and utilize relevant data over extended sequences, paving the way for significant advancements in natural language processing, time series analysis, speech recognition, and more. With the practical example presented, it is clear that implementing LSTM models is both accessible and effective, providing a starting point for exploring more complex problems.

The ongoing development in this field hints at a promising future, where LSTMs and their variants will evolve to address new challenges in our pursuit of more advanced artificial intelligence. The interaction of technology with human understanding deepens with each advance, and LSTMs stand at the center of this revolution.

Transformer Architecture

The Transformer architecture has revolutionized the field of natural language processing (NLP) and has been the foundation of many state-of-the-art models in artificial intelligence. Introduced by Vaswani et al. in the paper "Attention is All You Need" in 2017, Transformers have set a new standard by offering significant advantages over recurrent neural networks (RNN) and Long Short-Term Memory (LSTM) cells. In this chapter, we will explore the fundamental principles behind Transformers, their architecture, and how they are applied to various tasks in NLP.

What is a Transformer?

A Transformer is a type of neural network model that utilizes an attention mechanism instead of the typical sequential architecture of RNNs. This means that, instead of processing input in sequential order, a Transformer analyzes all the input simultaneously, allowing it to capture contextual relationships in the data more effectively. This capability has made Transformers exceptionally good for tasks that require an understanding of global context.

Fundamentals of the Transformer Architecture

The architecture of a Transformer is based on two main components: the encoder and the decoder. Below, we will define each of these components.

Encoder

The encoder is responsible for processing the input and generating feature representations that capture semantic information. The basic structure of an encoder includes:

- **Embedding Layer**: Converts input words into dense vectors. These vectors initialize the transformation process.

- **Attention Mechanism**: This is where the Transformer excels. It uses a mechanism called "Self-Attention" to determine how each word in the input relates to all other words. Each word receives attention based on its relevance to other words, allowing the model to focus on important contextual words.

- **Feedforward Layer**: After the attention mechanism, common dense layers (feedforward) are applied to further process the information.

- **Normalization and Residual**: Each attention and feedforward layer includes residual connections and batch normalization, facilitating better gradient propagation and helping learning to be more effective.

Each encoder consists of a series of these layers, allowing for a hierarchical construction of input representations.

Decoder

The decoder is responsible for generating the output from the encoder representations. Similar to the encoder, the decoder also includes:

- **Embedding Layer**: Converts output words (e.g., target language words in a translation task) into dense vectors.

- **Attention Mechanism**: In this case, the attention mechanism is divided into two. First, it uses self-attention over the generated part of the output to determine which previous parts of the output are relevant. Then, it uses another attention mechanism that focuses on the outputs from the encoder, allowing the decoder to "attend" to the original input.

- **Feedforward Layer**: Just like in the encoder, the decoder has dense layers that process the output information.

Another important point regarding the decoder is the use of a "mask" to prevent the prediction from depending on future words in the sequence during training.

Attention Mechanism

The attention mechanism is the heart of the Transformer architecture. It allows the model to focus on the most relevant parts of the input without treating all words equally. There are several types of attention mechanisms, but two of the most common are:

Self-Attention

Self-attention allows a word to relate to other words in the same sequence. Each word is transformed into a vector that will be used to calculate a weight.

Mathematically, the self-attention process involves three stages:

1. **Transformation into Keys, Values, and Queries**: Each input x is transformed into a *key vector* (Key, K), a *value vector* (Value, V), and a *query vector* (Query, Q) using learnable weight matrices.

$$Q = W^Q x, \quad K = W^K x, \quad V = W^V x$$

2. **Attention Calculation**: Attention is calculated through the multiplication of the query and key vectors, which is then passed through a softmax function to obtain normalized probabilities.

$$\text{Attention}(Q, K, V) = \text{softmax}\left(\frac{QK^T}{\sqrt{d_k}}\right) V$$

where d_k is the dimension of the keys. The division by $\sqrt{d_k}$ is used to avoid the attention values from becoming too large.

3. **Outputs**: Finally, the output is obtained as a weighted sum based on the values and computed attention.

Multi-Head Attention

One of the key innovations of Transformers is the use of Multi-Head Attention. Instead of performing a single attention operation, the model performs multiple attention operations in parallel. This allows the model to capture different representations and relationships in the input.

Multiple "attention heads" are performed, each generating its output. These outputs are then concatenated and projected into a common dimensional space.

Positional Encoding

Since Transformers lack the sequential nature of RNNs and LSTMs, they use a method called *Positional Encoding* to introduce information about the sequence of words. This is because neural networks have no other way of knowing the order of words within the input.

There are different ways to implement positional embeddings, but one of the most common is to use trigonometric functions to generate unique values for each position in the sequence:

$$PE(pos, 2i) = \sin\left(\frac{pos}{10000^{\frac{2i}{d_{model}}}}\right) \quad PE(pos, 2i + 1) = \cos\left(\frac{pos}{10000^{\frac{2i}{d_{model}}}}\right)$$

Where *pos* is the position in the sequence and i is the dimension. These functions ensure that each position in the sequence has a unique and unambiguous embedding vector.

Applications of Transformers

The Transformer architecture has been used in a wide range of applications in NLP, some of which include:

- **Machine Translation**: Models like Google Translate have adopted Transformers to provide more accurate and coherent translations between different languages.

- **Text Generation**: Models like GPT (Generative Pre-trained Transformer) use the Transformer architecture to autonomously generate text, tackling tasks ranging from creative writing to programming.

- **Sentiment Analysis**: Transformers are used to classify texts into positive, negative, or neutral sentiments, improving accuracy in this type of analysis.

- **Language Models**: BERT (Bidirectional Encoder Representations from Transformers) has enabled significant advancements in understanding context and relationships between words in a text, generating improvements in semantic search and other language comprehension tasks.

Example Implementation of a Transformer in Python

Below, we present a basic example of implementing a Transformer using TensorFlow and Keras. To simplify, we will design a Transformer architecture for a simple translation task.

Implementation Code

```python
import tensorflow as tf
from tensorflow.keras import layers, models

# Definition of dimensions
num_tokens = 10000
# Number of unique tokens in vocabulary
d_model = 128        # Dimension of embedding
num_heads = 8        # Number of attention heads
dff = 512            # Dimension of feedforward layer
dropout_rate = 0.1   # Dropout rate

# Attention Layer
class MultiHeadAttention(layers.Layer):
    def __init__(self, num_heads, d_model):
        super(MultiHeadAttention, self).__init__()
```

```python
            self.num_heads = num_heads
            self.d_model = d_model
            self.depth = d_model // num_heads

            self.wq = layers.Dense(d_model)
    # Weights layer for queries
            self.wk = layers.Dense(d_model)
    # Weights layer for keys
            self.wv = layers.Dense(d_model)
    # Weights layer for values

            self.dense = layers.Dense(d_model)  # Final layer

    def split_heads(self, x, batch_size):
            # Split the last dimension into multiple heads
            x = tf.reshape(x, (batch_size, -1, self.num_heads,
    self.depth))
            return tf.transpose(x, perm=[0, 2, 1, 3])

    def call(self, v, k, q, mask):
            batch_size = tf.shape(q)[0]

            query = self.wq(q)   # Multiply by weights
            key = self.wk(k)
            value = self.wv(v)

            query = self.split_heads(query, batch_size)
    # Split into heads
            key = self.split_heads(key, batch_size)
            value = self.split_heads(value, batch_size)

            # Scale dot product
            attn_logits = tf.matmul(query, key, transpose_b=
    True)
            attn_logits /= tf.math.sqrt(tf.cast(self.depth, tf.
```

```
      float32))
44
45          if mask is not None:
46              attn_logits += (mask * -1e9)
47
48          # Apply softmax to get attention scores
49          attention_weights = tf.nn.softmax(attn_logits, axis
   =-1)
50
51          # Apply attention to values
52          output = tf.matmul(attention_weights, value)
53
54          output = tf.transpose(output, perm=[0, 2, 1, 3])
   # Reorganize
55          output = tf.reshape(output, (batch_size, -1, self.
   d_model))  # Reshape back to original dimension
56
57          return self.dense(output)
   # Apply final dense layer
58
59  # Define the Transformer Model
60  def transformer(num_tokens, d_model, num_heads, dff,
   dropout_rate):
61      inputs = layers.Input(shape=(None,))
62      embedding = layers.Embedding(num_tokens, d_model)(
   inputs)
63      attention_output = MultiHeadAttention(num_heads,
   d_model)(embedding, embedding, embedding, None)
   # Apply attention
64      outputs = layers.Dense(num_tokens)(attention_output)
   # Final dense layer for output
65
66      return models.Model(inputs=inputs, outputs=outputs)
67
68  # Create the model and compile
```

```
69   model = transformer(num_tokens, d_model, num_heads, dff,
        dropout_rate)
70   model.compile(optimizer='adam', loss=
        'sparse_categorical_crossentropy')
71
72   # Model summary
73   model.summary()
```

Code Details

1. **Parameter Definition**: Some fundamental parameters such as the number of tokens, the embedding dimension, and the number of attention heads are defined.

2. **Multi-Head Attention Layer**: A multi-head attention layer is implemented as a class, managing the creation of queries, keys, and values for the attention mechanism. This layer enables the network to focus on different parts of the input in parallel.

3. **Transformer Model Definition**: The basic structure of the Transformer is constructed using the attention layer and a final dense layer for the output, allowing the model to produce output tokens.

4. **Model Compilation**: The model is compiled using the Adam optimizer and the sparse categorical cross-entropy loss function.

Conclusions

The Transformer architecture has marked a milestone in the development of natural language processing models. Its focus on attention and ability to capture long-range relationships have led to significant advances in tasks such as machine translation and sentiment analysis. As deep learning continues to evolve, Transformers will play a fundamental role in its advancement.

In the next chapter, we will further explore practical applications of Transformer models and how they have transformed entire industries through innovations in artificial intelligence.

Generative Models

Generative models are a fundamental approach in the field of artificial intelligence and machine learning. They are used to learn the distribution of data and generate new samples that are similar to instances of the original dataset. While discriminative models focus on predicting labels based on inputs, generative models seek to understand how data is generated and, from that understanding, are able to recreate new instances. This chapter will explore various types of generative models, with a special focus on Generative Adversarial Networks (GANs), their functioning, applications, and some of the challenges they face.

What are Generative Models?

In simple terms, a generative model is a type of model that tries to learn how data is distributed in a space, enabling models to generate new data that follows the same distribution. These models can be seen as functions that describe the probabilities of different data samples. Examples of areas where generative models are applied include:

- **Image Generation**: Creating new images that have similar characteristics to a training set.

- **Text Generation**: Writing coherent and relevant text, as done with language models.

- **Music Generation**: Composing musical pieces that follow certain styles or patterns.

The Difference between Generative and Discriminative Models

It is important to differentiate generative models from discriminative models:

- **Discriminative Models**: Focus on the decision boundary between different classes. For example, an image classifier that predicts whether an image is of a cat or a dog, based on the features that distinguish both classes.

- **Generative Models**: Try to understand how data is generated. For example, a generative model that has learned to produce images of cats and dogs from examples can generate new images of cats and dogs that it has never seen before.

This distinction is crucial because while discriminative models excel in classification, generative models offer much greater flexibility by allowing the creation of new data.

Generative Adversarial Networks (GANs)

One of the most prominent and revolutionary generative models is Generative Adversarial Networks (GANs). Introduced by Ian Goodfellow and his colleagues in 2014, GANs have made a significant impact on the generation of images, videos, and other types of data.

How Do GANs Work?

GANs consist of two neural networks that compete against each other: the generator and the discriminator. This approach can be better understood through the analogy of a game between two players:

1. **Generator**: This network takes as input a random noise vector (usually a vector of random numbers) and generates samples (e.g., images). Its goal is to create data that is indistinguishable from real data.

2. **Discriminator**: This network's task is to classify the samples as real (from the training set) or fake (generated by the generator). The goal of the discriminator is to maximize its accuracy in identifying real and fake data.

The training process of GANs is based on a competitive dynamic between these two networks:

- The generator tries to improve its ability to fool the discriminator.

- The discriminator tries to enhance its ability to distinguish between real and generated samples.

Training Process

The training of a GAN involves two stages:

1. **Training the Discriminator**: In this phase, the discriminator is presented with real samples alongside samples generated by the generator. The discriminator tries to correctly identify which are real and which are fake, adjusting its weights accordingly.

2. **Training the Generator**: After updating the discriminator, the generator is also updated. This network receives feedback based

on the discriminator's ability to classify the samples. The goal here is to maximize the probability that the discriminator classifies the generated samples as real. Mathematically, the generator's objective is to minimize the loss function that opposes that of the discriminator.

The process continues in an iterative training cycle until the generator produces samples that are undetectable by the discriminator.

Loss of GANs

The loss function used in GANs is very important and is defined for both networks as follows:

- Discriminator Loss (D):

$$L_D = -(E_{x \sim p_{data}(x)}[\log D(x)] + E_{z \sim p_z(z)}[\log(1 - D(G(z)))])$$

where $D(x)$ represents the probability that x is a real sample and $G(z)$ is the sample generated by the generator from the noise z.

- Generator Loss (G):

$$L_G = -E_{z \sim p_z(z)}[\log D(G(z))]$$

In this case, the generator seeks to maximize the probability that the discriminator classifies its samples as real.

Applications of GANs

GANs have been applied in various domains, showing their enormous versatility and potential:

- **Image Generation**: GANs are capable of creating high-quality images that appear real. Examples include generating human faces (using models like StyleGAN).

- **Data Augmentation**: They can be used to augment datasets in classification tasks, generating additional samples for rare classes.

- **Style Transfer**: GANs can apply the style of one image to another, such as in style transfer techniques, where, for example, an image can be drawn using the style of a famous painting.

- **Video Creation**: GANs have been used to generate video sequences, where the model tries to represent temporal context in addition to spatial.

Challenges in Training GANs

Despite their impressive capability, GANs present several challenges during training:

- **Instability in Training**: Maintaining the balance between the generator and the discriminator can be difficult. If one becomes too good, the other may not be able to learn properly.

- **Mode Collapse**: This phenomenon occurs when the generator produces a limited number of high-quality samples instead of capturing the diversity of the dataset. In other words, the generator learns to create a few variants that fool the discriminator, but does not generate enough variety.

- **Global and Local Balance**: Effective GAN training requires balancing global learning (capturing the distribution) with local learning (details and variations).

Example of Implementing a GAN in Python

Let's see how a simple GAN can be implemented using the Keras library in Python to generate images of handwritten digits from the MNIST dataset.

```python
1   import numpy as np
2   import matplotlib.pyplot as plt
3   from tensorflow import keras
4   from tensorflow.keras import layers
5
6   # Dimensions
7   latent_dim = 100  # Dimension of the noise vector
8
9   # Generator
10  def build_generator():
11      model = keras.Sequential()
12      model.add(layers.Dense(256, activation='relu',
        input_dim=latent_dim))
13      model.add(layers.BatchNormalization())
14      model.add(layers.Dense(512, activation='relu'))
15      model.add(layers.BatchNormalization())
16      model.add(layers.Dense(1024, activation='relu'))
17      model.add(layers.BatchNormalization())
18      model.add(layers.Dense(28 * 28, activation='tanh'))
19      model.add(layers.Reshape((28, 28, 1)))
20      return model
21
22  # Discriminator
23  def build_discriminator():
24      model = keras.Sequential()
25      model.add(layers.Flatten(input_shape=(28, 28, 1)))
26      model.add(layers.Dense(512, activation='relu'))
27      model.add(layers.Dropout(0.3))
28      model.add(layers.Dense(256, activation='relu'))
```

```python
29      model.add(layers.Dropout(0.3))
30      model.add(layers.Dense(1, activation='sigmoid'))
31      return model
32
33  # Build GAN model
34  generator = build_generator()
35  discriminator = build_discriminator()
36
37  discriminator.compile(optimizer='adam', loss=
    'binary_crossentropy', metrics=['accuracy'])
38
39  discriminator.trainable = False
    # Do not train the discriminator when training the
    generator

40  gan_input = layers.Input(shape=(latent_dim,))
41  generated_image = generator(gan_input)
42  gan_output = discriminator(generated_image)
43  gan = keras.models.Model(gan_input, gan_output)
44  gan.compile(optimizer='adam', loss='binary_crossentropy')
45
46  # Load MNIST dataset
47  (X_train, _), (_, _) = keras.datasets.mnist.load_data()
48  X_train = X_train.astype(np.float32) / 255.0
49  X_train = np.expand_dims(X_train, axis=-1)
50
51  # Training
52  def train_gan(epochs=1, batch_size=128):
53      for epoch in range(epochs):
54          # Train the discriminator
55          idx = np.random.randint(0, X_train.shape[0],
    batch_size)
56          real_images = X_train[idx]
57          noise = np.random.normal(0, 1, (batch_size,
    latent_dim))
```

```python
58          fake_images = generator.predict(noise)
59
60          d_loss_real = discriminator.train_on_batch(
    real_images, np.ones((batch_size, 1)))
61          d_loss_fake = discriminator.train_on_batch(
    fake_images, np.zeros((batch_size, 1)))
62          d_loss = 0.5 * np.add(d_loss_real, d_loss_fake)
63
64          # Train the generator
65          noise = np.random.normal(0, 1, (batch_size,
    latent_dim))
66          g_loss = gan.train_on_batch(noise, np.ones((
    batch_size, 1)))
67
68
    # If a certain number of epochs has passed, print the
    progress

69          if epoch % 100 == 0:
70              print(f"Epoch: {epoch}, Discriminator Loss: {
    d_loss[0]}, Generator Loss: {g_loss}")
71
72  # Run training
73  train_gan(epochs=10000)
74
75  # Generate and visualize images
76  def generate_images(num_images=10):
77      noise = np.random.normal(0, 1, (num_images, latent_dim)
    )
78      generated_images = generator.predict(noise)
79      plt.figure(figsize=(10, 10))
80      for i in range(num_images):
81          plt.subplot(5, 5, i + 1)
82          plt.imshow(generated_images[i, :, :, 0], cmap=
    'gray')
```

```
83          plt.axis('off')
84      plt.show()
85
86  generate_images(25)
```

Code Details

1. **Generator and Discriminator**: Two separate models are built. The generator takes the noise vector and transforms it into an image, and the discriminator classifies whether the image is real or generated.

2. **Compilation**: The discriminator is compiled first (ensuring it can be trained), and then the GAN model is built by combining both.

3. **Training**: Both models are alternately trained. In each iteration, the discriminator is trained with real and generated images, and the generator is trained to fool the discriminator.

4. **Image Generation**: After training, the effectiveness of the generator can be visualized by creating digit images.

Conclusions

Generative models, and particularly GANs, are transforming the way we understand and generate data. From creating images and music to generating text, these models have proven to be extremely versatile and powerful. However, they face significant challenges that, when addressed, will enable even greater advancements in artificial intelligence. As we explore more techniques in the upcoming sections, it is essential to consider the power and ethical implications of these models when implementing them in real-world applications.

Optimization Techniques

Optimization is a fundamental field in machine learning and, more specifically, in the context of deep learning. It involves adjusting the parameters of a model to minimize a loss function, thereby achieving better performance on specific tasks. This chapter will cover various optimization techniques, focusing on the different algorithms used in training models, as well as strategies to improve efficiency and effectiveness in learning.

Basic Concepts of Optimization

Optimization in deep learning refers to the continuous process of updating the weights of a neural network to minimize the loss function. The loss function, or cost function, measures how well the model performs on the specific task. A low loss function value indicates that the model is making predictions close to the actual values.

Mathematically, optimization seeks to find the parameters θ that minimize the loss function $L(\theta)$:

$$\hat{\theta} = \arg\min_\theta L(\theta)$$

Where $\hat{\theta}$ represents the optimal parameters to be found. To achieve this, we use optimization techniques that rely on the computation of the gradient of the loss function.

Gradient and Gradient Descent

The gradient of a multivariable function is a vector that points in the direction of the steepest ascent of the function. In the context of optimization, gradient descent is an algorithm for iterating toward the minimum of the loss function. The parameters are updated in the opposite direction of the gradient to descend the slope.

The update of the parameters θ is performed as follows:

$$\theta \leftarrow \theta - \eta \nabla L(\theta)$$

Where:

- η is the learning rate, a hyperparameter that controls the step size in each iteration.

- $\nabla L(\theta)$ is the gradient of the loss function with respect to the parameters.

Types of Gradient Descent

There are different variants of the gradient descent algorithm, each with its pros and cons:

Stochastic Gradient Descent (SGD)

Stochastic gradient descent updates the parameters using a single training example at each iteration. This reduces computation time but introduces variability in the trajectory toward the minimum:

$$\theta \leftarrow \theta - \eta \nabla L(\theta_i)$$

where i is an index representing an individual sample.

Advantages:

- Reduced training times.
- Can help escape local minima due to its noisy nature.

Disadvantages:

- The noisiness of the updates may lead to the algorithm not converging properly.

Batch Gradient Descent

This approach uses all examples in the training set to calculate the gradient before updating the parameters:

$$\theta \leftarrow \theta - \eta \nabla L(\theta)$$

where $L(\theta)$ is the loss calculated from the entire dataset.

Advantages:

- More stable results and convergence to local minima.
- Each step provides a "complete" view of the landscape of the loss function.

Disadvantages:

- It can be computationally expensive and slow for large datasets.

Mini-Batch Gradient Descent

A combination of SGD and batch gradient descent, mini-batch gradient descent divides the dataset into small batches, typically ranging from 32 to 256 samples:

$$\theta \leftarrow \theta - \eta \nabla L(\theta_{\text{batch}})$$

This variant allows for balance between the stability of full-batch descent and the speed of stochastic descent.

Advantages:

- Balance between computation time and stability in updates.
- Accelerates the computation process on large datasets by leveraging parallelization.

Disadvantages:

- Still requires tuning the learning rate and other hyperparameters.

Advanced Optimization Algorithms

As we progress in deep learning, it is crucial to have more sophisticated optimization algorithms that can accelerate convergence and improve model performance. Below are several of the most commonly used algorithms.

Adam (Adaptive Moment Estimation)

Adam is one of the most popular optimization algorithms due to its fast and effective performance on most deep learning tasks. It combines the advantages of two approaches: momentum-based gradient descent and adaptive learning rate gradient descent.

- **Features:**
  - Maintains an average of the gradients (first moment) and an average of the squared gradients (second moment) computed during training.
  - Updates parameters based on a combination of these moments.

The Adam update formula is:

$$m_t = \beta_1 m_{t-1} + (1 - \beta_1)g_t \quad v_t = \beta_2 v_{t-1} + (1 - \beta_2)g_t^2 \quad \hat{m}_t = \frac{m_t}{1-\beta_1^t} \quad \hat{v}_t = \frac{v_t}{1-\beta_2^t}$$

$$\theta \leftarrow \theta - \frac{\eta}{\sqrt{\hat{v}_t}+\diamond}\hat{m}_t$$

where:

- g_t is the gradient at time t.

- m_t and v_t are the first and second moments, respectively.

- β_1 and β_2 are the decay rates for the moments.

- $\diamond$ is a small term introduced to prevent division by zero.

RMSprop

RMSprop is another popular algorithm that adapts the learning rate. Unlike Adam, which uses both the first and second moments, RMSprop uses only the second moment:

$$v_t = \beta v_{t-1} + (1 - \beta)g_t^2 \quad \theta \leftarrow \theta - \frac{\eta}{\sqrt{v_t} + \diamond}g_t$$

RMSprop is especially useful in non-stationary problems where the learning rate may need to adjust during training.

Momentum

The Momentum algorithm introduces a kind of "inertia" in optimization, allowing the model to maintain its direction of movement:

$$v_t = \mu v_{t-1} + \eta \nabla L(\theta) \quad \theta \leftarrow \theta - v_t$$

Where:

- μ is the momentum term that controls the inertia.

With Momentum, the problem of noise in gradient descent is mitigated, allowing the model to move more smoothly along the surface of the loss function.

AdaGrad

AdaGrad adjusts the learning rate individually for each parameter, which is useful for handling rare features in the data. The parameter update is:

$$G_t = G_{t-1} + g_t^2 \quad \theta \leftarrow \theta - \frac{\eta}{\sqrt{G_t} + \diamond} g_t$$

Where G_t is the cumulative sum of the squares of the gradients.

The main disadvantage of AdaGrad is that its learning rate drastically reduces as training progresses, which can be the root cause of premature convergence.

Learning Strategies

In addition to selecting an optimization algorithm, a good learning strategy is also required. Here are some recommendations:

An Adaptive Learning Rate

Using a learning rate that adapts during training can be beneficial. For example, reducing the learning rate if the loss function does not improve over a specific number of epochs.

Learning Rate Decay

Implementing a learning rate decay, in which the rate decreases progressively as training continues, allows the model to explore the loss function more initially and then fine-tune parameters in the later stages.

Early Stopping

A technique that prevents overfitting involves stopping training early if no improvement in the loss function is observed on a validation set. This helps ensure that the model does not overfit the training data.

Regularization

Adding regularization techniques such as Dropout or L2 helps prevent overfitting and, in turn, optimizes the overall model performance.

Implementing an Optimization Algorithm in Python

To illustrate some of the above concepts, here is a basic example of how to implement the Adam algorithm in a neural network model using Keras:

```
1   import numpy as np
2   import tensorflow as tf
3   from tensorflow.keras import layers, models
4
5   # Generate a synthetic dataset
6   X_train, y_train = np.random.rand(1000, 20), np.random.
    randint(2, size=(1000, 1))
7
8   # Model definition
9   model = models.Sequential()
10  model.add(layers.Dense(64, activation='relu', input_shape=(
    20,)))
11  model.add(layers.Dense(1, activation='sigmoid'))
```

```
12
13  # Compile the model using Adam
14  model.compile(optimizer='adam', loss='binary_crossentropy',
       metrics=['accuracy'])
15
16  # Train the model
17  model.fit(X_train, y_train, epochs=10, batch_size=32)
```

Code Details

1. **Synthetic Data Creation**: A simple random dataset is generated with 1000 samples and 20 features.

2. **Model Creation**: A neural network is defined with one hidden layer of 64 neurons and an output layer that produces a binary prediction.

3. **Model Compilation**: Adam is used as the optimizer, which facilitates managing the adaptive learning rate.

4. **Training**: The model is trained for 10 epochs with a batch size of 32.

Conclusions

Optimization is a critical and complex aspect of deep learning. Understanding the different optimization techniques and algorithms can make a significant difference in model performance. From stochastic gradient descent and its variants to advanced methods like Adam and RMSprop, approaches vary in their effectiveness depending on the task and model architecture. Learning strategies and regularization techniques complement these algorithms, helping models scale and generalize effectively to new data.

As we continue to explore deep learning, a solid understanding of optimization techniques will provide the necessary foundation for building more robust and accurate models in real-world applications.

Regularization

Regularization is a fundamental technique in machine learning and deep learning used to prevent a model from overfitting to the training data. When a model is too complex, it adapts not only to the general trends in the data but also to the noise and fluctuations in the training data. This results in poor performance when the model is evaluated on unseen data. In this chapter, we will explore various regularization techniques, their fundamentals, how they are implemented, and practical examples in Python.

What is Overfitting?

Overfitting occurs when a model learns the details and noise of the training dataset too well, instead of effectively generalizing the patterns that can apply to new data. This translates into a model that performs poorly on the validation or test dataset, as it cannot correctly predict new instances that are not part of the training set.

Visualization of Overfitting

Imagine we are training a regression model to predict the price of a house based on certain attributes (such as size, number of rooms, etc.). If our model is simple, it may not learn the underlying patterns in the data, resulting in poor performance (this state is called underfitting).

On the contrary, if we create a very complex model (for example, high-degree polynomials), the model may fit every data point in the training set, but it will not be able to generalize effectively to new data. Visually, this can be observed in a graph where the fitting curve passes very close to all points, compared to a curve that captures the general trend of the data without strictly fitting every point.

Regularization Techniques

There are several regularization techniques available to mitigate overfitting. Some of the most common include:

L1 and L2 Regularization

L1 and L2 regularization are widely used techniques to add a penalty term to the model's loss function during training.

L2 Regularization (Ridge)

L2 regularization, also known as Ridge regularization, adds a penalty term that is proportional to the square of the magnitude of the model coefficients.

The loss function with L2 regularization is defined as:

$$L(\theta) = L_{\text{original}}(\theta) + \lambda \sum_{i=1}^{n} \theta_i^2$$

Where:

- $L_{\text{original}}(\theta)$ is the original loss function (such as mean squared error).

- λ is a hyperparameter that controls the strength of the regularization (also known as the regularization factor).

- θ_i are the model weights.

The effect of L2 regularization is to make the model weights smaller, preventing them from fitting too closely to the training data.

L1 Regularization (Lasso)

L1 regularization, also known as Lasso, adds a penalty term that is proportional to the absolute value of the model coefficients:

$$L(\theta) = L_{\text{original}}(\theta) + \lambda \sum_{i=1}^{n} |\theta_i|$$

L1 regularization has the unique property of being able to drive some of the model weights exactly to zero, which essentially aids in feature selection.

Dropout

Dropout is another popular technique mainly used in neural networks. During training, Dropout randomly "turns off" a percentage of neurons in each layer while feeding inputs to the network. This prevents neurons from becoming too reliant on each other and promotes greater robustness in the network.

For example, if we set a 50% Dropout, during each training iteration, about half of the neurons will randomly be deactivated. As a result, the model learns to generalize and does not rely on a specific set of neurons.

Data Augmentation

Data augmentation is a technique by which new instances of data are generated from the existing ones. Instead of training a model on a single dataset, variations of images, text, or any other data are created to form a larger training set.

Examples of data augmentation for images include rotations, translations, scaling, and brightness changes. This not only increases the amount of available data for training, but also helps the model learn invariant features in the data.

Early Stopping

Early stopping is a regularization technique that halts the training of the model before overfitting occurs. During training, we monitor the loss function on a validation set. If there is no improvement over a specific number of epochs (referred to as "patience"), training is stopped to prevent the model from overfitting the training data.

Implementing Regularization in Python

Below are examples of using L1 and L2 regularization in a neural network model using Keras:

L2 Regularization in Keras

```python
1  import numpy as np
2  from tensorflow import keras
3  from tensorflow.keras import layers
4  from tensorflow.keras.regularizers import l2
5
6  # Generate a synthetic dataset
7  X_train = np.random.rand(1000, 20)
8  y_train = np.random.randint(2, size=(1000, 1))
9
10 # Model definition
11 model = keras.Sequential()
12 model.add(layers.Dense(64, activation='relu',
       kernel_regularizer=l2(0.01), input_shape=(20,)))
13 model.add(layers.Dense(1, activation='sigmoid'))
14
15 # Compile the model
16 model.compile(optimizer='adam', loss='binary_crossentropy',
       metrics=['accuracy'])
17
18 # Train the model
19 model.fit(X_train, y_train, epochs=10, batch_size=32)
```

L1 and L2 Regularization in Keras

```python
1  from tensorflow.keras.regularizers import l1_l2
2
3  # Model definition with L1 and L2
4  model = keras.Sequential()
5  model.add(layers.Dense(64, activation='relu',
```

```
    kernel_regularizer=l1_l2(l1=0.01, l2=0.01), input_shape=(
    20,)))
 6  model.add(layers.Dense(1, activation='sigmoid'))
 7
 8  # Compile the model
 9  model.compile(optimizer='adam', loss='binary_crossentropy',
    metrics=['accuracy'])
10
11  # Train the model
12  model.fit(X_train, y_train, epochs=10, batch_size=32)
```

Dropout in Keras

```
 1  # Model definition with Dropout
 2  model = keras.Sequential()
 3  model.add(layers.Dense(64, activation='relu', input_shape=(20
    ,)))
 4  model.add(layers.Dropout(0.5))  # 50% Dropout
 5  model.add(layers.Dense(1, activation='sigmoid'))
 6
 7  # Compile the model
 8  model.compile(optimizer='adam', loss='binary_crossentropy',
    metrics=['accuracy'])
 9
10  # Train the model
11  model.fit(X_train, y_train, epochs=10, batch_size=32)
```

Early Stopping in Keras

```
 1  from tensorflow.keras.callbacks import EarlyStopping
```

```
 2
 3  # Define EarlyStopping
 4  early_stopping_monitor = EarlyStopping(
 5      monitor='val_loss',
        # Monitor the loss function on the validation set
 6      patience=3,
        # Stop if no improvement over 3 epochs
 7      restore_best_weights=True # Restore the best weights
 8  )
 9
10  # Train the model with EarlyStopping
11  model.fit(X_train, y_train, epochs=100, validation_split=0.2,
            callbacks=[early_stopping_monitor])
```

Conclusions

Regularization is a vital tool in the machine learning arsenal. By using regularization techniques, it is possible to build models that generalize better to unseen data, avoiding overfitting issues that can arise with excessively complex models.

Each regularization technique has its advantages and disadvantages, and the appropriate choice largely depends on the nature of the dataset and the specific model being used. By understanding and applying these techniques, engineers and data scientists can significantly enhance the performance of their models, achieving better results in real-world tasks. Regularization not only contributes to the robustness and effectiveness of the model but is also crucial for the long-term sustainability of artificial intelligence implementations.

Natural Language Processing I

Natural Language Processing (NLP) is a sub-discipline of artificial intelligence that deals with the interaction between computers and humans through natural language. Its goal is to enable computers to understand, interpret, and generate human language in a way that is valuable. From practical applications like chatbots, machine translation, and sentiment analysis, NLP has become fundamental in the development of intelligent systems that effectively interact with users. In this chapter, we will explore the essential concepts of NLP, basic techniques, and some fundamental models in its implementation.

Introduction to Natural Language Processing

Human language is inherently complex and filled with subtleties. For a computer to work with natural language, it must break it down into comprehensible and usable elements. This includes interpreting not only the words but also their grammar, syntax, semantics, and the context in which they are used. Nowadays, NLP is applied in various areas, such as:

- **Chatbots**: Conversational systems that interact with users in natural language.

- **Machine Translation**: Tools that translate texts from one language to another, such as Google Translate.

- **Sentiment Analysis**: Processes that determine the emotions or attitudes of speakers from texts, widely used in the analysis of comments and reviews.

The ability to understand and manipulate natural language allows machines to provide richer and more satisfying experiences to users.

Text Representation for Neural Networks

One of the first steps in any natural language processing task is transforming text into a format that a neural network can process. This involves converting words and sentences into vectors of numbers. Below, we will discuss two widely used techniques for text representation.

One-Hot Encoding

The **One-Hot Encoding** technique is a simple way to represent words in a vector space. In a One-Hot Encoding scheme, each word in the vocabulary is represented as a vector. This vector is the same size as the total number of words in the vocabulary, with each word represented as a vector of zeros and a single one. For example, if we have a vocabulary of three words: ["cat", "dog", "bird"], the One-Hot Encoding of these words would be:

- "cat": [1, 0, 0]

- "dog": [0, 1, 0]

- "bird": [0, 0, 1]

Although One-Hot Encoding is easy to implement, it has several disadvantages. First, the representation is very sparse, as most values are zeros. Additionally, it does not capture similarities between words; for example, "cat" and "dog" do not share any information in the space.

Word Embeddings

To address the limitations of One-Hot Encoding, **Word Embeddings** were developed, which represent words in a lower-dimensional continuous feature space. Techniques like Word2Vec, GloVe, and FastText generate dense vectors for words, where semantically similar words are closer to each other in the vector space. For example, the words "king" and "queen" might have vectors that are closer together than the words "king" and "stone."

Word2Vec

Word2Vec is a Word Embeddings model based on two approaches: the Continuous Bag of Words (CBOW) model and the Skip-Gram model.

- **CBOW**: This model predicts a central word given its context of adjacent words. For example, given the sentence "the cat is on the", the model might predict the word "roof."

- **Skip-Gram**: In this approach, a central word is taken to predict its contexts. Using the same previously mentioned sentence, the model would use the word "cat" to predict "the", "is", "on", and "the".

Both models generate dense representations for words that encapsulate meanings and relationships.

Basic Models for NLP

Once the text is properly represented, models can be built for specific NLP tasks. Below, we will explore some of the basic models commonly used in natural language processing.

Recurrent Neural Networks (RNNs)

Recurrent Neural Networks (RNNs) are designed to work with sequential data, such as natural language. Unlike traditional neural networks, RNNs have connections that allow them to maintain information about previous states, providing a short-term memory. This is particularly useful in language processing, where context is critical.

Functioning of RNNs

RNNs implement a structure where the output of a cell is fed back into the network for the next input. Mathematically, this can be expressed as:

$$h_t = \text{activation}(W_h h_{t-1} + W_x x_t + b)$$

Where:

- h_t is the hidden state at time t.
- x_t is the input at time t.
- W_h and W_x are weight matrices for the hidden and input connections, respectively.
- b is a bias.

RNNs are powerful, but they suffer from issues like gradient vanishing and explosion, which can hinder their training on long sequences.

Long Short-Term Memory (LSTM)

LSTMs are a variant of RNNs designed to mitigate the issues of gradient vanishing. They introduce gate mechanisms that allow the model to decide when to remember or forget information.

Structure of an LSTM

The LSTM unit consists of three main gates:

- **Input Gate**: Controls the amount of information fed into the hidden state.

- **Forget Gate**: Decides what information is discarded from the hidden state.

- **Output Gate**: Controls what information is output from the LSTM cell.

This design allows LSTMs to capture long-term dependencies in sequences, making them particularly useful in NLP tasks and text generation.

Bidirectional Recurrent Neural Networks (Bi-RNN)

Bi-RNNs are an extension of RNNs that consist of two RNN layers: one processes the sequence in the standard order and the other processes it backward. This allows the network to access context from both directions, which can enhance performance in tasks like machine translation and sentiment analysis.

Problems and Limitations of RNNs

Despite their advantages, RNNs and their variants have disadvantages. They struggle with long sequences due to gradient vanishing and long training times. For this reason, more advanced models, such as **Transformers**, have been developed to address these limitations and have proven to be extremely effective in NLP tasks.

Conclusions

In this chapter, we have explored the basic concepts of Natural Language Processing. From text representations to models like RNNs and LSTMs, we have covered the foundations necessary to tackle NLP tasks. As we progress into exploring more sophisticated and state-of-the-art techniques in the upcoming chapters, it is crucial to solidify these basic concepts, as they form the foundation upon which NLP models are built in real-world applications. A solid understanding of these techniques will enable us to harness the power of natural language in its multiple applications.

Natural Language Processing II

Natural Language Processing (NLP) has evolved significantly in recent years, driven by advances in deep learning and new architectures such as Transformer-based models. In this chapter, we will focus on the impact of Transformers on NLP, as well as modern language models like BERT, GPT, and T5. We will also explore advanced techniques such as fine-tuning, transfer learning, and the adaptation of pre-trained models in various practical applications.

Transformers and Their Impact on NLP

The introduction of the Transformer architecture has revolutionized the way NLP tasks are approached. Unlike recurrent neural networks (RNNs) that process information sequentially, Transformers use an attention mechanism that allows for parallel processing of input. This not only significantly speeds up training time but also improves the model's ability to capture distant contextual relationships in the text.

Transformers are composed of two main components: the encoder and the decoder. In the context of NLP, these components are used for tasks such as machine translation, text generation, and language understanding.

Self-Attention

One of the most innovative aspects of the Transformer architecture is the self-attention mechanism. Through this process, the model evaluates the importance of each word in the context of other words in the sentence. This allows the model to consider not only adjacent words but also those that are more distant, thereby enhancing its understanding of the text.

Example of Self-Attention

Consider the sentence: "The black cat sat on the sofa." An attention mechanism can help the model understand that "cat" and "sofa" are related. The self-attention assesses the interactions between these words, allowing the model to assign different levels of importance when generating a prediction or response.

Modern Language Models

BERT (Bidirectional Encoder Representations from Transformers)

BERT, developed by Google, is a Transformer-based model that has revolutionized NLP. One of its main innovations is that it is bidirectional, meaning it takes into account both the preceding and following context of a word in a sentence. This contrasts with unidirectional models that only consider either the preceding or the following context.

Pre-training and Fine-tuning

BERT is trained on two pre-training tasks:

1. **Masked Language Modeling**: In this approach, random words in a sentence are masked. The model must predict these words based on the context provided by the remaining words.

   Example: "The cat is on the [MASK]." The model must predict the word "sofa."

2. **Next Sentence Prediction**: This second objective helps the model understand the relationship between two sentences, which is crucial for comprehension tasks.

Once pre-trained, BERT can be fine-tuned on specific tasks such as text classification, question answering, and sentiment analysis, adjusting its parameters based on a smaller, more specific dataset.

GPT (Generative Pre-trained Transformer)

GPT, developed by OpenAI, is another significant advance in NLP that is based on the Transformer architecture. Unlike BERT, GPT is a unidirectional model, meaning it only considers preceding context when generating text.

Text Generation

GPT's main strength lies in its ability to generate coherent and contextually relevant text. By providing the model with a prompt, GPT can continue writing smoothly, making it a powerful tool for tasks such as content writing, dialogue generation, and storytelling.

Example of Text Generation with GPT

If we provide a starting line such as "It was a dark and stormy night," GPT might continue with something like: "A shadow slipped between the trees, its silhouette barely visible under the dim light of the moon." GPT's ability to extrapolate from limited context is one of its most notable traits.

T5 (Text-to-Text Transfer Transformer)

T5, also from Google, is a versatile model based on the notion that all NLP tasks can be reformulated as text-to-text translation tasks. For instance, a text classification task can be viewed as "Is this text positive or negative?" which transforms into texts representing the answer.

Training Steps

T5 is pre-trained on a wide variety of NLP tasks and then fine-tuned for specific tasks. This allows it to tackle diverse tasks, from language translation to summarization.

Advanced Techniques in NLP

Fine-tuning

Fine-tuning is the process of adjusting a pre-trained model on a new specific dataset to improve its performance on a particular task. For example, after pre-training BERT on large text corpora, it can be fine-tuned on a dataset for sentiment detection in product reviews.

Transfer Learning

Transfer learning refers to the technique of using a model trained on one task and applying it to another task. By transferring what has been learned from a related task, models can achieve better results with less training data. For example, a model trained for sentiment analysis can be adapted for topic classification.

Adaptation of Pre-trained Models

Adapting a pre-trained model involves adjusting its weights and architectures to meet specific requirements of a new application. This may include modifying output layers or introducing new activation functions to better fit the new dataset.

Practical Applications in NLP

The implementation of these modern NLP models in real-world applications has been remarkable. Here are some key applications:

- **Intelligent Chatbots**: Systems that use BERT and GPT to interact with users more naturally and effectively.

- **Machine Translation**: Translation models that use T5 to provide more accurate and contextual translations in multiple languages.

- **Sentiment Analysis**: Analysis tools that use BERT to classify opinions on social media and product reviews.

- **Content Generation**: GPT is used in applications that automatically generate text for articles, blogs, and more.

Implementing Modern Models in Python

Below is a simple example of how to use the `transformers` library from Hugging Face to load and use a pre-trained BERT model for a classification task:

```python
from transformers import BertTokenizer,
    BertForSequenceClassification
from transformers import Trainer, TrainingArguments
import torch

# Load the tokenizer and pre-trained BERT model
tokenizer = BertTokenizer.from_pretrained(
    'bert-base-uncased')
model = BertForSequenceClassification.from_pretrained(
    'bert-base-uncased')

# Define input data
texts = ["I love this product, it's amazing!",
    "I don't like it at all, it's a disaster."]
labels = [1, 0]  # 1 for positive, 0 for negative

# Tokenize the texts
inputs = tokenizer(texts, padding=True, truncation=True,
    return_tensors="pt")
inputs['labels'] = torch.tensor(labels)

# Prepare training parameters
training_args = TrainingArguments(
    per_device_train_batch_size=2,
    num_train_epochs=3,
    logging_dir='./logs',
)
```

```
24  # Train the model
25  trainer = Trainer(
26      model=model,
27      args=training_args,
28      train_dataset=inputs
29  )
30
31  trainer.train()
```

Code Details

1. **Load the Tokenizer and Model**: We use `BertTokenizer` and `BertForSequenceClassification` from the `transformers` library to load the pre-trained BERT model.

2. **Define Input Data**: We create a list of texts along with their respective labels.

3. **Tokenization**: We transform the texts into a format that the model can process.

4. **Training**: We use the `Trainer` class to train the model on our data.

Conclusions

Natural Language Processing has been transformed by advances in architectures such as Transformers, which have allowed for a deeper and more effective modeling of language. Models such as BERT, GPT, and T5 not only improve accuracy on specific tasks but also offer new opportunities for innovative applications in the real world. By combining techniques like fine-tuning and transfer learning, developers can harness the power of these pre-trained models to build intelligent systems that understand and generate natural language coherently and relevantly. As technology continues to advance, we can expect NLP to play an increasingly central role in our interaction with artificial intelligence systems.

Computer Vision I

Computer vision, also known as artificial vision, is a field of study within artificial intelligence that deals with how computers can be programmed to gain a visual understanding of the world. The main goal of computer vision is to develop algorithms and models that enable machines to interpret and process images or video sequences similarly to how humans do. This chapter will explore the fundamentals of computer vision, its real-world applications, and the classical models of convolutional neural networks (CNNs) that have marked a milestone in this field.

Introduction to Computer Vision

Computer vision encompasses a wide range of tasks, such as object detection, image segmentation, classification, and pattern recognition. Just like the human sense of sight, which allows us to perform everyday tasks like identifying a familiar face, reading a book, or recognizing a car, computer vision seeks to enable machines to perform these tasks automatically.

An essential aspect of computer vision is its ability to learn from visual data. With the advent of deep learning techniques and neural networks, specifically convolutional networks, computer vision has made significant progress, achieving levels of accuracy that rival those of humans in certain tasks.

Applications of Computer Vision

The applications of computer vision are vast and diverse. Some of the most notable include:

- **Facial Recognition**: Used in security and authentication systems, facial recognition allows for the identification and verification of a person's identity by analyzing their facial features.

- **Autonomous Vehicles**: Autonomous vehicles use computer vision to detect and recognize traffic signs, pedestrians, and other vehicles, enabling them to navigate safely in various conditions.

- **Medicine**: In the healthcare field, computer vision techniques are applied to analyze medical images, such as X-rays or MRIs, helping to detect diseases and conditions with greater precision.

- **Agriculture**: Computer vision is used in precision agriculture to monitor crops, detect pests, and optimize resource use.

- **Robotics**: Robots equipped with computer vision systems can perform tasks more efficiently, ensuring a more interactive and adaptive environment.

Computer vision is undoubtedly a field that is redefining the way we interact with the technology around us.

Image Representation in Neural Networks

To understand how neural networks can work with images, it's essential to comprehend how images are represented digitally. In general, an image consists of a matrix of pixels. Each pixel can contain values that represent the amount of light (or color) at that point in the image.

Color Representation

In most cases, images are represented in color using an RGB (Red, Green, Blue) representation system. In this scheme, each pixel is defined by three values:

- **R**: Red color intensity.
- **G**: Green color intensity.
- **B**: Blue color intensity.

For example, a white pixel would have the RGB values (255, 255, 255), while a black pixel would have (0, 0, 0). The mixture of different intensities of these three colors allows for the creation of a wide variety of colors.

Image Dimensions

When discussing images in terms of machine learning and neural networks, it is common to refer to the image dimensions. A color image of size $width \times height$ will be represented as a three-dimensional matrix with dimensions $(height, width, 3)$, where the "3" represents the color channels (RGB).

Image Preprocessing

Before images are introduced into a neural network, certain preprocessing steps need to be performed, which may include:

- **Resizing**: Changing the dimensions of the image to match the expectations of the model (e.g., 224x224 pixels, which is the size commonly used for many pretrained models).

- **Normalization**: Adjusting pixel values to fall within a more manageable range, often between 0 and 1, to facilitate the training process.

- **Data Augmentation**: Applying random transformations to images (such as rotations, cropping, or brightness changes) to create variations of the original dataset, thereby improving the model's generalization capability.

Convolutional Neural Networks (CNNs)

Convolutional Neural Networks (CNNs) have proven to be extremely effective in tasks of computer vision. Their architecture is particularly well-suited for processing data in the form of images due to their convolutional layers, which allow for the detection of local features within images.

Basic Structure of a CNN

A CNN typically consists of several layers, including:

- **Convolutional Layers**: These layers apply filters (or kernels) to the input image, performing convolution operations. Each filter is capable of detecting specific features, such as edges or textures. The result of the convolution is a feature map that represents the activation of that feature in the image.

- **Activation Layers**: Activation layers, such as ReLU (Rectified Linear Unit), are applied after convolutional layers to introduce non-linearities into the model, enabling it to learn more complex relationships.

- **Pooling Layers**: These layers are used to reduce the dimensionality of feature maps, retaining the most relevant information. Typically, max pooling or average pooling operations are used.

- **Fully Connected Layers**: Towards the end of the network, fully connected layers take the outputs from the convolutional and pooling layers and convert them into the final output of the model, which could be a classification or object detection.

Example Architecture of a CNN

Below is a basic diagram of how a CNN might be structured for image classification:

```
[Input Image]
--> Convolution --> [Feature Map]
                    -- ReLU --
                    -- Pooling --

[Feature Map]
--> Convolution --> [Feature Map]
                    -- ReLU --
                    -- Pooling --

[Feature Map]
--> Flatten --> [Feature Vector]

[Feature Vector]
```

```
--> Fully Connected --> [Final Classification]
```

Loss Function and Optimization

The loss function is used during training to assess how well the model is performing. In classification tasks, the most common loss function is cross-entropy. The weights and biases of the network are adjusted through gradient descent and its variants.

Example Implementation of a CNN in Python

Below is an example of how to implement a simple CNN using the Keras library in Python to classify images from the MNIST dataset, which contains images of handwritten digits:

```
1   import numpy as np
2   import matplotlib.pyplot as plt
3   from tensorflow import keras
4   from tensorflow.keras import layers
5
6   # Load the MNIST dataset
7   (X_train, y_train), (X_test, y_test) = keras.datasets.mnist
    .load_data()
8   # Reshape images
9   X_train = np.expand_dims(X_train, axis=-1).astype('float32'
    ) / 255.0
10  X_test = np.expand_dims(X_test, axis=-1).astype('float32')
    / 255.0
11
12  # Define the CNN architecture
13  model = keras.Sequential([
```

```
14      layers.Conv2D(32, kernel_size=(3, 3), activation='relu'
  , input_shape=(28, 28, 1)),
15      layers.MaxPooling2D(pool_size=(2, 2)),
16      layers.Conv2D(64, kernel_size=(3, 3), activation='relu'
  ),
17      layers.MaxPooling2D(pool_size=(2, 2)),
18      layers.Flatten(),
19      layers.Dense(128, activation='relu'),
20      layers.Dense(10, activation='softmax')
  # 10 classes for digits 0 to 9
21  ])
22
23  # Compile the model
24  model.compile(optimizer='adam', loss=
  'sparse_categorical_crossentropy', metrics=['accuracy'])
25
26  # Train the model
27  model.fit(X_train, y_train, epochs=5, batch_size=64,
  validation_data=(X_test, y_test))
28
29  # Evaluate the model
30  test_loss, test_acc = model.evaluate(X_test, y_test)
31  print(f'Test accuracy: {test_acc:.4f}')
```

Code Details

1. **Loading and Preprocessing Data**: The MNIST dataset is loaded, and the dimensions are expanded to include the color channel (in this case, 1 for grayscale images). Images are normalized to fall within the range of 0 to 1.

2. **Model Construction**: The CNN architecture is defined with convolutional layers, pooling layers, and fully connected layers.

3. **Model Compilation**: The Adam optimizer and cross-entropy loss are used.

4. **Training**: The model is trained using the training set and validated with the test set.

5. **Evaluation**: The model's accuracy is assessed on the test set.

Conclusions

Computer vision is a fascinating and constantly evolving field that offers numerous opportunities across various industries. By understanding the fundamentals of image representation and convolutional neural networks, it is possible to build models that can perform complex visual interpretation tasks. As we progress into the following chapters, we will continue exploring more advanced techniques and innovative architectures that are driving computer vision into the future. The confluence of artificial intelligence with the ability to "see" the world opens up a plethora of possibilities that are transforming our interaction with technology and the environment surrounding us.

Computer Vision II

In the previous chapter, we explored the fundamentals of computer vision and the basic architectures of Convolutional Neural Networks (CNNs). In this chapter, we will dive into more advanced techniques that improve the performance of computer vision models. We will address concepts such as Transfer Learning and Fine-Tuning, as well as analyze advanced CNN models like ResNet and DenseNet, and their relationship with vision Transformers. Finally, we will explore object detection techniques such as U-Net, YOLO, and SSD, all designed to solve specific tasks in real-world problems.

Improving Performance with Transfer Learning and Fine-Tuning

Transfer Learning is a technique that allows us to leverage a pre-trained model on large datasets to solve specific tasks with a smaller dataset. This is especially useful in computer vision, where collecting and labeling large volumes of data can be costly and labor-intensive.

Concept of Transfer Learning

The fundamental idea behind Transfer Learning is to take a model that has already learned useful features from a domain (for example, classifying images with a thousand classes in the ImageNet dataset) and adapt it to a new task. Pre-trained models can extract features that are relevant for a wide range of applications, allowing a new model to be trained faster and with fewer data.

Fine-Tuning Process

Once a pre-trained model is chosen, the next step is the Fine-Tuning process. This process involves two stages:

1. **Freezing Layers**: In most cases, the initial layers of the pre-trained model that have already learned general features (such as edges and textures) are frozen, and only the upper layers that are more adapted to the new task are trained.

2. **Unfreezing Layers**: Then, some of the lower layers can be unfrozen to allow the model to learn more task-specific features.

This approach maximizes the use of pre-trained weights, fine-tuning them to be more specific to the new classification or segmentation task.

Example of Transfer Learning in Keras

Below is an example where we use a pre-trained model, in this case, VGG16, to classify images from a small dataset:

```
1  from tensorflow import keras
2  from tensorflow.keras import layers
```

```
3   from tensorflow.keras.applications import VGG16
4
5
    # Load the pre-trained VGG16 model without the
    classification layers

6   base_model = VGG16(weights='imagenet', include_top=False,
    input_shape=(224, 224, 3))
7
8   # Freeze the base layers
9   for layer in base_model.layers:
10      layer.trainable = False
11
12  # Create a new model
13  model = keras.Sequential([
14      base_model,
15      layers.Flatten(),
16      layers.Dense(256, activation='relu'),
17      layers.Dense(10, activation='softmax')
    # Assuming we have 10 classes
18  ])
19
20  # Compile the model
21  model.compile(optimizer='adam', loss=
    'sparse_categorical_crossentropy', metrics=['accuracy'])
22
23  # Training
24  model.fit(train_data, train_labels, epochs=5, batch_size=32
    )
```

Advanced Models: ResNet and DenseNet

The ResNet and DenseNet architectures are two significant innovations in the field of computer vision. These architectures were designed to address common problems in training deep neural networks, such as vanishing and exploding gradients.

ResNet (Residual Network)

The central idea behind ResNet is the introduction of "residual paths." Instead of learning direct functions (the output of each layer is the input to the next), ResNet allows layers to learn the difference between the input and the desired output, facilitating the training of very deep networks.

Concept of Residual Blocks

A typical residual block in ResNet looks like this:

```
Input --> Conv --> ReLU --> Conv --> Add --> ReLU --> Output
```

The "Add" function allows the original input to be added to the output of the block, facilitating gradient propagation more effectively. This solves the overfitting problem and allows the network to be trained with many more layers without losing learning capacity.

DenseNet

DenseNet further improves upon the idea of connectivity. Instead of just allowing information to flow through residual connections, each layer in DenseNet receives inputs from all previous layers. This means that feature information from prior layers is reused at each stage.

Advantages of DenseNet

1. **Fewer Parameters**: By reusing features, DenseNet can be more efficient in terms of the number of parameters it needs to function correctly.

2. **Better Gradient Propagation**: The dense connection allows for better gradient propagation, resulting in more efficient training.

Example Code to Use ResNet50 in Keras

```
1  from tensorflow.keras.applications import ResNet50
2
3
   # Load the pre-trained ResNet50 model without the
   classification layers

4  base_model = ResNet50(weights='imagenet', include_top=False
   , input_shape=(224, 224, 3))
5
6  # Freeze the base layers
7  for layer in base_model.layers:
8      layer.trainable = False
9
10 # Create a new model with an additional dense layer
11 model = keras.Sequential([
12     base_model,
13     layers.GlobalAveragePooling2D(),
14     layers.Dense(10, activation='softmax')  # 10 classes
15 ])
16
17 # Compile the model
```

```
18  model.compile(optimizer='adam', loss=
    'sparse_categorical_crossentropy', metrics=['accuracy'])
19
20  # Training
21  model.fit(train_data, train_labels, epochs=5, batch_size=32
    )
```

Object Detection

Object detection is a crucial task in computer vision that focuses on identifying and locating objects within an image or video. Various architectures and models have been designed for this task, with some of the most popular being U-Net, YOLO, and SSD.

U-Net

U-Net is a model primarily used for image segmentation and is famous in biomedical applications. It is based on an encoder-decoder architecture, where the encoder captures detailed information, and the decoder uses it to identify object segmentation.

Structure of U-Net

U-Net consists of two parts:

1. **Contracting Path**: Convolutional and pooling layers are used to reduce the resolution and capture high-level features.

2. **Expanding Path**: Transposed convolution layers are used to increase the image resolution, which is concatenated with features from the contracting phase.

This allows the model to utilize high-resolution data during the segmentation process, resulting in more accurate final segmentation maps.

YOLO (You Only Look Once)

YOLO is an object detection model based on the idea of making predictions in a single network, instead of going through multiple stages. This makes YOLO highly efficient and fast.

How YOLO Works

YOLO divides the input image into an S x S grid and, for each cell in the grid, predicts a fixed number of bounding boxes along with a confidence score. The network also predicts classes for each box. This approach allows detecting multiple objects in an image in real-time.

SSD (Single Shot Detector)

SSD is another object detection model that is based on a similar approach to YOLO but with a different design. Like YOLO, SSD combines detection and classification prediction in a single network but uses multiple scales to detect objects of different sizes.

Implementation of YOLO in Python

Below is a simplified code to use YOLO with the OpenCV library:

```
1  import cv2
2  import numpy as np
```

```
3
4   # Load YOLO model and weights
5   net = cv2.dnn.readNet("yolov3.weights", "yolov3.cfg")
6   layer_names = net.getLayerNames()
7   output_layers = [layer_names[i[0] - 1] for i in net.
    getUnconnectedOutLayers()]
8
9   # Load the image
10  image = cv2.imread("image.jpg")
11  height, width, _ = image.shape
12
13  # Prepare image for YOLO
14  blob = cv2.dnn.blobFromImage(image, 0.00392, (416, 416), (0
    , 0, 0), True, crop=False)
15  net.setInput(blob)
16  outs = net.forward(output_layers)
17
18  # Process predictions
19  for out in outs:
20      for detection in out:
21          scores = detection[5:]
22          class_id = np.argmax(scores)
23          confidence = scores[class_id]
24          if confidence > 0.5:  # Minimum confidence
25              center_x = int(detection[0] * width)
26              center_y = int(detection[1] * height)
27              w = int(detection[2] * width)
28              h = int(detection[3] * height)
29
30              # Bounding box coordinates
31              x = int(center_x - w / 2)
32              y = int(center_y - h / 2)
33
34              # Draw the box
35              cv2.rectangle(image, (x, y), (x + w, y + h), (0
```

```
       , 255, 0), 2)
36
37  # Show result
38  cv2.imshow("Image", image)
39  cv2.waitKey(0)
40  cv2.destroyAllWindows()
```

Conclusions

In this chapter, we have explored advanced techniques in computer vision that significantly improve the performance of models. Transfer Learning and Fine-Tuning have proven effective in leveraging pre-trained models, while architectures like ResNet and DenseNet enable the training of deeper networks without losing learning capacity. Additionally, object detection has been addressed through models like U-Net, YOLO, and SSD, demonstrating how neural networks can segment and detect objects in images effectively.

As we continue our journey in the world of artificial intelligence, these advanced computer vision techniques will be fundamental in tackling real-world challenges and building applications that transform our interaction with technology. The ability of machines to "see" and understand their environment is changing the way we live and work, and it will be exciting to see how this field evolves in the coming years.

Ethical Considerations

Artificial intelligence (AI) is rapidly transforming the way we live, work, and communicate. From virtual assistants on our phones to algorithms that predict behaviors and make decisions in record time, the impact of AI is profound and omnipresent. However, with this power comes significant responsibilities and the need to address crucial ethical questions. In this chapter, we will discuss the ethical considerations in artificial intelligence, highlighting social and economic impacts, biases in models, and the importance of developing responsible and fair AI.

Social and Economic Impacts

The development and implementation of AI systems have the potential to revolutionize entire sectors, from healthcare to education and industry. However, these changes come with concerns about how they will affect society and the economy.

Job Displacement

One of the most discussed concerns is the impact of AI on employment. As automation advances, many fear that certain jobs will become obsolete. For example, the development of autonomous vehicles could significantly affect truck and taxi drivers. While AI can increase efficiency and reduce costs, these improvements could lead to massive job displacement.

However, it is essential to consider that AI can also create new jobs in areas such as software development, data management, and analytics. The key lies in the adaptability and retraining of the workforce. Educators and public policymakers must work together to provide training in digital and technical skills, preparing individuals for emerging opportunities.

Access and Inequality

Another important consideration is access to technology. AI has the potential to improve lives, but it can also deepen existing inequalities. Instead of advising the most disadvantaged, AI systems can disproportionately benefit those already privileged. For example, digital health tools may assist resourceful communities, leaving behind more vulnerable communities that lack internet access.

It is essential to take measures to ensure that AI technologies benefit everyone, regardless of geographical location, educational level, or socioeconomic status. This involves policies that promote digital inclusion and accessibility in education, health, and labor markets.

Biases in Machine Learning Models

Artificial intelligence models are far from neutral. Since these models are trained on historical data, they can inherit and amplify existing biases in that data. This can lead to unfair and discriminatory outcomes affecting minority and underrepresented groups.

Examples of Bias

A notorious example of bias in AI is found in hiring systems. If a model is trained on data from resumes and past hires that are predominantly from a specific demographic group (e.g., white men), the model may favor those candidates, even if there are equally qualified candidates from underrepresented groups. This perpetuates the lack of diversity in the workplace and reinforces harmful stereotypes.

Another example can be found in facial recognition systems, where studies have shown that some algorithms have higher error rates when classifying faces of people of color compared to faces of white individuals. This can lead to severe consequences, including disproportionate surveillance and racial profiling.

Mitigating Bias

Mitigating bias in AI requires a multidimensional approach. Some steps include:

- Collecting more diverse and representative data for model training.
- Implementing independent auditors to evaluate and review existing models for biases and errors.
- Promoting transparency in the development of AI models, allowing third parties to examine data, algorithms, and results.

The Need for Responsible AI

As artificial intelligence becomes more integrated into our daily lives, responsibility in its design and application becomes essential. Ethics in AI should not be a secondary topic, but rather a fundamental consideration at all stages of development and deployment.

Ethical Principles

Emerging from discussions across the tech and academic communities, the ethical principles of AI include:

- **Transparency**: Users should understand how and why automated decisions are made. Opacity in algorithms can lead to distrust among users.

- **Fairness**: AI systems should be designed to be fair and equitable, avoiding biased outcomes that could harm certain groups.

- **Accountability**: Clear mechanisms should be established for accountability in cases where an AI system causes harm, whether through errors or harmful decisions.

- **Privacy**: The collection and use of personal data should be done with respect for individuals' privacy, ensuring the security and confidentiality of information.

Creating an Ethical Framework

A robust ethical framework is needed to guide both developers and companies in creating responsible AI systems. This may include:

- Collaboration between ethicists and data scientists in AI

development teams.

- Workshops and training on ethics for engineers and AI experts.
- Establishing AI ethics committees within organizations to assess the impact of emerging technologies.

Conclusions

Ethical considerations in artificial intelligence are fundamental to ensuring that technology is developed and implemented in a way that benefits society as a whole. From mitigating biases to inclusion and fairness, it is imperative that all stakeholders involved in AI work together to create a future where technology is not only innovative but also responsible and ethical.

As we move into the era of AI, the challenge is clear: to build systems that are not only powerful and efficient but also respect and promote human values. With a firm focus on ethics and justice, we can ensure that artificial intelligence becomes a positive and transformative force for the common good.

Technical Challenges and the Future of Deep Learning

Deep learning has revolutionized the field of artificial intelligence, allowing us to tackle complex problems and develop remarkable applications ranging from autonomous driving to natural language processing. However, like any emerging technology, deep learning faces a series of technical challenges that must be addressed to improve its effectiveness and efficiency. Throughout this chapter, we will examine these challenges and explore future trends in deep learning, reflecting on how it will impact our world.

Current Limitations of the Technology

Data Requirements

One of the most significant challenges in deep learning is the need for large amounts of high-quality data for model training. Although deep learning models have demonstrated their ability to learn complex representations from data, they often require massive datasets to generalize effectively. This raises several issues:

- **Data Collection**: Gathering and labeling large datasets can be costly and labor-intensive. In some cases, it may be nearly impossible to obtain enough representative data, such as in the case of rare diseases in medical research.

- **Data Quality**: Not only is quantity important, but also quality. Biased or poorly labeled data can lead to ineffective or unfair models. For example, a model trained with images of cars that only show a specific brand may not adequately recognize other vehicles.

Computational Resources

Training deep learning models, especially those with complex architectures, requires considerable computational resources. This includes:

- **Specialized Hardware**: GPUs (graphics processing units) are essential for effective training, but not all organizations have access to this type of hardware. This limits research and development capacity in smaller institutions or developing countries.

- **Training Time**: Deep learning models can take anywhere from hours to days or even weeks to train, depending on the model's complexity and the quality of the hardware used. This can limit the rate of experimentation, as each iteration requires a significant investment of time and resources.

Model Interpretability

As deep learning models become increasingly complex, transparency and interpretability become ever more critical issues. The opacity of how decisions are made by AI models can generate distrust among users and undermine technology adoption. Two important aspects include:

- **Black Box**: Deep learning models are often regarded as "black boxes," meaning it is not easy to understand the internal process that led to a particular decision. This is a critical issue in sensitive applications, such as medical diagnosis or credit decision-making.

- **Need for Explainability**: There is a growing demand for models that are not only accurate but also provide understandable explanations for their decisions. This involves developing methods to interpret the outputs of convolutional and recurrent models in ways that meet ethical and legal standards.

Future Trends in Deep Learning

As we confront these challenges, the future trends in deep learning appear promising. There are several directions in which the field is advancing, potentially changing how we implement and utilize this technology.

Transfer Learning and Continuous Learning

Transfer learning allows a model trained on one task to deduce information and knowledge from other tasks. Instead of starting from scratch, pre-trained models can be adapted to specific applications through a process called Fine-Tuning. This not only saves time in terms of training but also reduces the need for large volumes of data in many situations.

On the other hand, continuous learning refers to a model's ability to incrementally adapt to new information without forgetting what it has previously learned. This approach is extremely relevant in dynamic environments where data is constantly changing, such as object recognition in the real world.

Generative Models

Generative models, such as Generative Adversarial Networks (GANs), have been an exciting area of research in recent years. They allow for the generation of new data based on patterns learned within a training dataset. The future could see advancements in the ability of these models to generate synthetic data that rivals real data, thus opening new avenues for creating useful datasets in areas where data is scarce.

Federated Learning

Federated learning is a technique that enables machine learning models to be trained on multiple devices without the need to centralize data, which is essential from a privacy perspective. This approach can be particularly useful in developing AI systems that handle sensitive data, such as health information. With federated learning, models can benefit from data from diverse sources without compromising confidentiality, thereby addressing concerns about data security and ownership.

Innovations in Architecture

The development of new model architectures, such as Transformers, has revealed that they are well-equipped to handle both structured and unstructured data. Undoubtedly, the Transformer architecture has revolutionized natural language processing and may also impact computer vision and other areas. With each new research advancement, we can expect models that are more efficient, scalable, and easier to interpret.

The Role of Ethics in the Future of Deep Learning

As we consider the evolution of deep learning, it is essential not to lose sight of ethical considerations. Decisions made in the design, training, and implementation of AI models must align with justice and fairness.

- **Responsible Development**: With the growing use of models in everyday applications such as autonomous driving or surveillance, creating a framework that guides the ethical development of algorithms will be crucial to avoid harm.

- **Multidisciplinary Collaboration**: The future of deep learning will benefit from greater collaboration between engineers, social scientists, and ethics experts. This will allow for a holistic view in the development of models that are not only technically effective but also socially responsible.

Conclusions

Deep learning remains one of the most fascinating areas of artificial intelligence. However, to continue advancing, we must address the technical challenges facing the discipline. As technology evolves, future trends suggest a promising path toward more efficient, ethical, and adaptable models.

By considering the intersection of technology and ethics, along with the development of continuous innovations, we can harness the potential of deep learning to create a future in which artificial intelligence serves humanity justly and equitably. Whether through improving real-world applications or exploring new methodologies, the future of deep learning is as exciting as it is crucial.